Stop Trying to
Fix Policing

I0091988

Critical Perspectives on Race, Crime, and Justice

Series Editor: Tony Gaskew, University of Pittsburgh, Bradford

This book series seeks interdisciplinary scholars whose work critically addresses the racialization of criminal justice systems. Grounded within the connective space of history, the nuances of race continue to define the standard of how justice is applied throughout policing, courts, and correctional systems. As such, this series is open to examine monographs and edited volumes that critically analyze race from multiple narratives—sociopolitical, cultural, feminist, psychosocial, ecological, critical theory, philosophical—along criminal justice lines. The Critical Perspectives on Race, Crime, and Justice book series speaks to the significant scholarship being produced in an era where race continues to intersect with crime and justice.

Titles in the series

Stop Trying to Fix Policing: Lessons Learned from the Front Lines of Black Liberation by Tony Gaskew

Race, Education, and Reintegrating Formerly Incarcerated Citizens: Counterstories and Counterspaces edited by John R. Chaney and Joni Schwartz

Law Enforcement in the Age of Black Lives Matter: Policing Black and Brown Bodies, edited by Sandra E. Weissinger and Dwayne A. Mack

Stop Trying to Fix Policing

Lessons Learned from the Front Lines of Black Liberation

Tony Gaskew

LEXINGTON BOOKS
Lanham • Boulder • New York • London

Published by Lexington Books
An imprint of The Rowman & Littlefield Publishing Group, Inc.
4501 Forbes Boulevard, Suite 200, Lanham, Maryland 20706
www.rowman.com

6 Tinworth Street, London SE11 5AL, United Kingdom

Copyright © 2021 by The Rowman & Littlefield Publishing Group, Inc.

All rights reserved. No part of this book may be reproduced in any form or by any electronic or mechanical means, including information storage and retrieval systems, without written permission from the publisher, except by a reviewer who may quote passages in a review.

British Library Cataloguing in Publication Information Available

Library of Congress Control Number: 2020948486

ISBN 978-1-4985-8950-5 (cloth)
ISBN 978-1-4985-8952-9 (pbk)
ISBN 978-1-4985-8951-2 (electronic)

Contents

Acknowledgments

On July 23, 1991, my son Adonis Gaskew was introduced into this universe with an *oriki*. On February 5, 2019, my father Walter Gaskew made his transition into the land of my ancestors through an *isinku*. There have never been two more important living beings in my life. Every single page in this book is dedicated to their shared visions of the Black diaspora.

Introduction

Policing is just a hustle. A greed injected American racist hustle. A hustle that depends on the mass exploitation and extinction of Black bodies as capitol. Never lose sight of this universal truth. Much of policing's appeal is based on white money, white myths, and white miscreants. The myth that policing is dangerous. The myth that policing is an effective solution for public safety. The myth that policing faces an actual, significant risk of being unfairly prosecuted, fired, or sued. The myth that the Black body is the villain. The myth that policing can be reformed. The policing hustle is based predominantly on lies and mythologies that are rooted in a history of American white supremacy and both macro and micro frames of direct and structural violence. James Baldwin (1966, para. 17) in *A Report from Occupied Territory* once said, "The police are simply the hired enemies of this population. They are present to keep the Negro in his place and to protect white business interests, and they have no other function." This remains as true today as it was in 1966, and once again fifty four years later, Black people in America are questioning the legitimacy of policing. However, the Pan-Afrikan (Black) diaspora has grown, and its goals, strategies, and tactics for Black resistance have evolved, weaponing themselves physically, culturally, spiritually, and intellectually to fight against police violence.

What we now clearly understand is that the millions of unlawful stop and frisks around the country are not only assaults on basic civil rights but an *erotic police ritual* designed to humiliate, shame, and colonize the manhood of its victims and, by extension, an attempt to assassinate the willpower of Black resistance (Curry, 2017). What do you do with an institution whose core function is the control, exploitation, and elimination of Black people in America? Big money and countless miscreants push this agenda. It's easy to understand when annually over \$100 billion is placed directly into policing budget coffers, combined with another half a trillion dollars in post-secondary endowments, where countless police practitioners and professors alike are more than happy to spread *coproproganda*. However, what Black people in America now understand is the more you peel back the layers, the more you begin to uncover just how fragile, weak, and vulnerable the policing culture is today. The institution of policing is holding on for its life.

When it comes to finding solutions—any solution that centers on ending police violence against the Black diaspora in America—white liberals embrace lies, untruths, and fairy tales. They want to be told unicorn stories about good cops and bad apples falling from trees, body cameras, implicit bias training, procedural justice, place-based policing, focused deterrence, and predictive policing and about how Black police chiefs, Black prosecutors, and Black judges are going to fix policing. They want to be comforted and reassured that everything is going to be okay and that with a steadfast intersectionalist worldview, policing will be reformed someday. In fact, they demand that these same lies be fed to the Black masses across America. White liberal progressives will fund countless criminal justice feel-good projects across the academy, happily co-opt any Black social movement or Black liberal activist willing to establish a GoFundMe account, and pour tons of cash and time into electing any congressional representative or district attorney across the nation that campaigns against cash bail or prosecuting misdemeanor marijuana cases, in order to simply maintain their own policing power over the Black narrative. You see, the truth sits at the heart of white fear, white identity, and white survival, as it relates to the role that all white people play in the institution of policing in America. The truth is there is no hope for reform, reconciliation, or healing when it comes to the Black diaspora and its relationship to policing and many white liberals in America.

You see, I speak my truths as my father spoke his truths. My dad explained that by my very birthright and spiritual inheritance, I was going to be a vanguard of justice. He explained that my life's purpose was to engage in a war with white supremacy and that policing in America was the armed wing of white supremacy. He made me understand that the *Black radical tradition* is a 200,000-year-old spiritual inheritance that weaves the ontological journey of Black humanity, Black survival, and Black power. It is the collective consciousness of the Black cultural experience, born as the vanguards of human life. It is the totality of truth, justice, balance, harmony, order, righteousness, and reciprocity, passed on by through rituals, from one generation of Blackness to the next, creating an endless cycle of cosmic dark matter. As a soldier in the Black Power Movement, my dad spoke the language of critical race theory (CRT) long before Derrick Bell (1984, 1987, 1988, 1990, 1992a,b) advanced the term throughout the academy. My dad explained that white supremacy must be fought face-to-face and that I would be entering the battlefield of policing in order to fight white supremacy. I listened.

By January 2000, I had spent nearly sixteen years in policing, learning its systemic and exploitable weaknesses and fighting white supremacy, as my father had prophesized. However, another conversation with my dad would change the course of my life. My dad asked if I had finished what I started in policing. When I explained that the war against white supremacy never ends, he laughed and told me how proud he was of me and of my sacrifice for Black liberation. He then advised me to prepare myself to widen the battlefield in fighting anti-Black systems of oppression. He instructed me to finish graduate school and to weaponize my intellect, expanding the war against the armed wing of white supremacy from the streets to the classrooms. My dad understood Ture's (1967a) vision of Black power and the role education plays in organizing the masses from the *unconscious to the conscious*.

Fast forward to June 2020 and I'm a tenured full professor of criminal justice, Faculty Affiliate in Afrikana Studies, and director of criminal justice at the University of Pittsburgh, Bradford. In fact, as a Black male, I'm part of a very small fraternity that makes up less than 2 percent of all full professors within the academic discipline of criminal justice (Greene, Gabbidon, & Wilson, 2018). I weaponized my intellect, immersing myself into publications, presentations, and revolutionary Black radical tradition actions that aggressively challenged every narrative created by the policing culture to criminalize the Black diaspora in America. Although my father has since transitioned into the world of my ancestors, he continues to bring his wisdom to me through the Afrikan ritual of meditation. Thus, I continue to dedicate every moment of my career in the academy fighting white supremacy, following Ture's (1967b) empathic call by ensuring that every single student, staff member, faculty, or administrator that I come into contact with is educated not only on the poisonous nuances of systemic racism and white supremacy within American policing but also on the inevitable reality that policing will eventually be dismantled and abolished.

Thus, over the last five decades, I have been part of an organic critical autoethnographic journey, listening to the voices of Black people across America—a lot of Black people—asking them one basic question "How do we get policing out of our lives?" Young, old, men, women, straight, gay, lesbian, and transgender. Neighborhood store owners, barbers, the homeless, schoolteachers, prosecutors, police officers, gang members, musicians, janitors, college students, bartenders, poets, vendors, construction workers, street hustlers, feminists, activists, and formerly and currently incarnated people. At malls, barbershops, grocery stores, parks, college campuses, liquor stores, coffee shops, protests and demonstrations, grassroots community meetings, and gun ranges and inside carceral facilities of oppression. From Oakland,

NYC, Los Angeles, Chicago, Atlanta, Detroit, New Orleans, Birmingham, Washington, DC, Baltimore, Philadelphia, Houston, St. Louis, Jackson, Memphis, Cleveland, and Buffalo.

You see, within the Black radical tradition, I listened to people share their life's journey under the oppressive state of American policing, stories that seem to sit at the core of what Baldwin (1961) described in *The Negro in American Culture* as both Black rage and Black liberation. As a Pan-Afrikanist, with a revolutionary spirit taught to me as a student of Kwame Ture (1967, 1971, 2003) and El-Hajj Malik El-Shabazz (Haley, 1964), I listened to their nuanced and rich stories, which were framed by both personal experiences and the oral histories of police encounters passed through their family and friends alike. While listening to their voices, I proudly digested the genius of Jalil Muntaqim (2010) in *We Are Our Own Liberators*, when he humbly reminds all of us that one of the most important facets of understanding Black liberation is to first establish national programs for decolonization. You see, during my conversations, I noted that some Black people supported a need for the police and justified it by expressing a fear, whether real or imagined, of "life without policing." While others insisted that although they despise a police presence in their own community, they feel powerless to fight them or remove their occupying presence from their neighborhoods. After listening over and over again to many of these stories, which bravely narrated the political and cultural burden described by Kwame Ture (2003) in *Ready for Revolution* and the transgenerational nihilism depicted by Cornel West (2001) in *Race Matters*, I've come to the conclusion that colonization, as a subset of the American brand of white supremacy, has been the worst psychic violence ever perpetrated on the Black collective (Ture, 1967).

My conversations with abolitionists and supporters of abolitionist groups across America helped construct my understanding of not only the nuanced approaches used in abolitionism today but how they successfully levy their grassroots influence to compel policy initiatives that have opened the door for police abolition. However, these conversations also demonstrated to me how white supremacy permeates these abolitionist movements as well. CRT applies to abolitionism in America. Although this is a discussion for another book, my readers must clearly understand that a significant part of abolitionism energy is wasted keeping white members and white allies happy. In addition, pacifism became a problematic theme at times. At the end of the day, for some white abolitionists, it's still about how to maintain their own power, control, and influence over the aboriginal. Lost in this sea of white funded abolition movements is the quest for Black power and Black liberation. Abolition movements offer several sound tactics, as I note throughout my book, but these movements will never result in dismantling American policing. Ultimately, it's not in their best interests (Gaskew, 2014a,b, 2018, 2020a).

My conversations with Black police officers also shed light on new platforms of research within CRT. A critical race examination of Black policing in America extends the dialogue of how Black police officers perceive their role, if any, in Black liberation. With no evidence to suggest otherwise, Black police officers or better yet, the Black policing culture, readily sustain(s) the permanence of white supremacy within the systemic institution of policing. Although it's very easy to fall into the white liberal trap of blaming this phenomenon on tough-on-crime legislation, implicit bias, broken windows, or some theoretical framework involving Black self-threats or institutional norms, it all comes down to colonization.

However, my conversations with advocates and supporters of the Black Liberation Army (BLA), the Nation of Islam (NOI), the Black Panther Party for Self-Defense (BPP), and the Republic of New Afrika (RNA), some incarcerated, some formerly incarcerated, and some still clandestine or hidden in plain sight shaped the core body of ideological, philosophical, political, and cultural scholarship for this book. Peniel Joseph (2007) in *Waiting 'Til the Midnight Hour: A Narrative History of Black Power in America* argued that the Black radical tradition, or what we know as the Black Power Movement, was the "template for restructuring society" (p. xviii). I believe the Black radical tradition is the template for police abolition. Their ancestral words of wisdom made what is perceived as a very daunting task—the dismantling of policing in America—seem as calm, as smooth, and still as breathing during meditation (Gaskew, 2020a,b). As such, the voice of this BLA supporter set the tone of my scholarly journey into police abolition:

> The Black radical tradition laid the groundwork, the blueprint, for restructuring Black reality. I challenge and reject any Eurocentric interpretation of my culture, politics, history, and life within my Black experience. The only role policing serves in America is to make feeble attempts to translate the language of my Black experience to the white masses, as crimes, in order to feed their fear of the aboriginal. Thus, policing and anyone who supports policing is the enemy of Black people. Policing and anyone who supports policing has always been the enemy of Black people. Policing and anyone who supports policing will always be the enemy of Black people. The question has never been about Black liberation. The question has always been about how to deal with those that oppose Black liberation.

In keeping with this same spirit of Black liberation and Black resistance, in every single page of this chapter, I capitalize the *B* in *Black* while leaving the *w* in *white* in lowercase. Of course, today this choice is no longer just a demonstration of cultural and political power; it has become literary mantra of many style guides and dictionaries today. I know this will make some of my white readers uncomfortable, but what I've discovered in my journey to a path of truth and justice is that it's okay to sometimes feel uncomfortable. At the deepest levels of human growth and potential is our collectively shared fear of being inferior, that is, the pain and suffering associated with our unwillingness to understand that all living beings are connected and that all of our actions and deeds are reciprocal in nature. Using all of our senses, the constructs of white supremacy and the *wrong view*, rooted in fear and anger, must be exposed, destabilized, and destroyed. It is at this point that the doors of Black liberation are fully opened. Tiptoeing around white supremacy and the differences guided by its self-preserving mythical constructs is unhealthy and only leads down a path of systemic pain, suffering, and humiliation.

However, I cannot overemphasize that every word in this chapter is spoken under the universal Afrikan language of an earthy, mystic, and cosmological love. Love that confronts, love that resists, love that heals, and love that liberates. Unraveling the messy entanglement that white supremacy and its many tentacles have had on the thoughts, feelings, and dreams of all people will require a revolutionary truth. *Our Pan-Afrikan truth*. It will take pealing back the many layers of pain, suffering, and lies associated with white supremacy to unveil the origins of justice. *Our Pan-Afrikan justice*. It will take recovering our ancestral memories through the process of rituals, in order to regain our balance. *Our Pan-Afrikan balance*. It will take a focused understanding that only through a collective voice, will harmony be achieved. *Our Pan-Afrikan harmony*. It will take the energy and willpower of the masses to bring together a collective order. *Our Pan-Afrikan order*. It will take a wisdom that is centered on always doing the right thing. *Our Pan-Afrikan righteousness*. And finally, it will take a deep understanding that the universe is created on the basis of cause and effect or what we know as *Ari*. *Our Pan-Afrikan reciprocity*. It will take a warrior's spirit to save all beings, to balance all desires, to master all truths, and to liberate all sufferings.

During my journey trying to unravel the metaphysical web of police abolition—if the term "abolition" is what we really want to call it—as one of less than ten Black full professors of criminal justice in the entire nation and having walked down this intellectual road several times before (Gaskew, 2014a,b, 2018), I could hear the timeless ancestral voice of Ture (1967a) in my soul, always humbly reminding me of the lessons he learned in the 1960s as one of the most revolutionary living beings to ever walk the planet (Williams, 2002). Ture (1967b) insisted that the masses, the Black masses, must lead any revolution for liberation. That the revolution behind Black liberation was not going to come from a charismatic Black politician, a Black intellectual, or a Black entertainer, but from the collective synergy of the Black masses. Ture

(1967b) reminded us that without the support of the Pan-Afrikan masses, any revolution for liberation would be doomed for failure. This book unearths the voices of the Black radical tradition.

You see, while sitting at Reading Terminal Market in Philadelphia back in 2017, catching my thoughts and sipping on a cup of green tea and honey, I was listening to a conversation between three elderly Black men and was reminded of the universal purity of Black soul. That cosmological connection between science and spirituality that only old Black wisdom has secured. One of the Black men was pointing at a uniformed Philadelphia police officer, who was also a Black male, standing in line waiting to pay for his meal, and the elderly Black gentleman very loudly and clearly stated, "They think hiring more Blacks is a solution. Well it aint. Motherfuckers are all the same. This shit don't fool nobody." The other two gentlemen seemed to agree, and one uttered, "Fuck him, as Black people we need to stop trying to fix the police." It was obvious that the police officer they were directing these comments toward heard them and acknowledged his awareness by awkwardly staring in their direction. The three elderly Black men stared right back at him with contemptuous fearlessness, and after a few seconds, the police officer looked the other way (Gaskew, 2020a).

All I could think about at that moment was my own father, and just how special old Black men are as vanguards of truth and liberation. As a Black man in America who lived to be nearly ninety years old in a country saturated in Jim Crow and white supremacy, my father shared his revolutionary wisdom with me. This moment, which I understand now was a ritual, brought me back home to my ancestry (Gaskew, 2014a,b, 2018, 2020a,b). These three elderly Black men in Philadelphia echoed a theme I heard my entire life: *stop trying to fix policing.* I heard it from Black healthcare professionals, FedEx drivers, and airline employees. I heard it from Derrick Bell (1992a) in *Faces at the Bottom of the Well.* I heard it from Jamil Abdullah al-Amin (1969) in *Die Nigger Die,* The Black Liberation Army (1971) in *Message to the Black Movement: A Political Statement from the Black Underground,* Robert L. Williams (1962) in *Negroes with Guns,* Kwame Nkrumah (1968) in *Handbook of Revolutionary Warfare,* Marimba Ani (1994) in *Yurugu: An African-Centered Critique of European Cultural Thought and Behavior,* Assata Shakur (1987) in *Assata: An Autobiography,* Charles Cobb Jr. (2015) in *This Nonviolent Stuff'll Get You Killed: How Guns Made the Civil Rights Movement Possible,* Akinyele Omowale Umoja (2014) in *We Will Shoot Back,* Russell Schoatz (2013) in *Maroon the Implacable,* and Kuwasi Balagoon (2019) in *A Soldier's Story: Revolutionary Writings by a New African Anarchist.*

I heard it from Salathiel Thompson (2016, 2020b) in *The United States of America vs. The United States of America,* Mumia Abu-Jamal (2016) in *We Want Freedom: A Life in the Black Panther Party*, Thomas Sankara (1988) in *Thomas Sankara Speaks: The Burkina Faso Revolution 1983-1987*, Jeffrey Hass (2010) in *The Assassination of Fred Hampton: How the FBI and the Chicago Police Murdered a Black Panther*, and Angela Davis (2005) in *Abolition Democracy*. I heard it from Kwame Ture (1967) in *Black Power: The Politics of Liberation*, Clarence Williams (1971) in *The Destruction of Black Civilization*, Franz Fanon (1967) in *Wretched of the Earth*, and Eldridge Cleaver (1968) in *Soul on Ice*. I heard it from John Henrik Clarke (1998) in *Christopher Columbus and the African Holocaust: Slavery and the Rise of European Capitalism*, Carter G. Woodson (1933) in *The Mis-Education of the Negro*, Huey Newton (1972) in *To Die for the People*, Frances Cress Welsing (1992) in *The Isis Papers*, George Jackson (1970) in *Soledad Brother*, and Amos Wilson (1998) in *Blue Print for Black Power*. I heard it from Elijah Muhammad (1965) in *Message to the Blackman in America*, Martin Luther King Jr. (1968) in *Why We Can't Wait*, El-Hajj Malik El-Shabazz (1964) in *The Autobiography of Malcom X*, W. E. B. DuBois (1899) *in Philadelphia Negro*, and Marcus Garvey (1927) in *The Tragedy of White Injustice*. Pan-Afrikan voices have always spoken the language of police abolition. Maybe now it's time to translate the words into action.

   This book is critical of pathological nonviolence, which is the white liberal tactical mantra of how abolitionism is packaged for Black consumer intersectionalist consumption today. The institution of policing cannot be dismantled by Black Lives Matter (BLM) demonstrations and protests. It cannot be dismantled by obediently absorbing rubber bullets, baton blows, and tear gas. It cannot be dismantled by watching, recording, and begging a police officer to take his knee off the neck of a breathless Black body. It cannot be dismantled by prostrating one's body during the playing of the national anthem or taking knee with your favorite police chief, prosecutor, or twitter activist. Policing cannot be dismantled by the act of defunding. The institution of policing can only be dismantled through the ritual of revolution. Without revolution, there is no police abolition. This book is about how the Black radical tradition in America envisions the ritual of revolution, aimed toward dismantling the institution of policing. It is about Black people synergizing the science and spirituality of self-defense. It is about Black people collectively exercising self-determination and organizing politically, culturally, and metaphysically for a life without policing. The stakes have never been higher. If the Black diaspora in America fail to take action, our children will bear the shame, subjugation, and humiliation of our transgenerational deaths at the hands of state violence. If we succeed, we will fulfill our mandate as the human vanguards of the universe. As such, this book seeks to contribute to the development of Black liberation and the liberation of all oppressed people across the planet who are fighting against state violence. There is nothing unilateral about the liberation of Pan-Afrikan people in America (Gaskew, 2020b).

In this book, I touch on five interwoven rituals for revolution, voiced within the Black radical tradition, as necessary and sufficient to dismantle the institution of policing in America: *learning to speak the language of police abolition, unfriending policing, decolonizing the state narrative, community self-determination*, and *Black armed resistance*. These rituals work collectively to expose the inherent systemic weaknesses of American policing, the policing culture, and the policing state. These rituals are also a living and breathing testament of Black resistance in America. Policing is nothing more than a science experiment in state violence, whose actors are collectively fearful, fragile, and feeble; thus policing must be understood, debunked, and dismantled by exploiting all of its collective paleness. The ritual science of revolution must be used to abolish policing. As such, the criticisms in this book directed toward policing—and there are many—never refer to an individual police officer but to the systemic and collective nature of policing in America. It is fundamentally important to draw this distinction. Police abolition will require revolutionary, radical, and fearless Black thought and Black action. This shared commitment is woven into the Pan-Afrikan cultural DNA. I hope this book inspires a new standard of revolution toward Black liberation. One that makes American policing obsolete.

Chapter 1

Learning to Speak the Language of Police Abolition

In 1973, as a nine-year-old, I was standing on the corner of 117th & Michigan Ave, which is on the far Southside of Chicago in the Roseland neighborhood known today as the "Wild 100s," waiting on a CTA bus to go home after school. This was a very popular location not only because of the busy bus stop but because there was a store, we called them candy stores, adjacent to the street corner. There were maybe 100 or so kids on the corner and directly in front of me there were two white teenage boys leaning on a fire alarm box. One of them suddenly pulled the fire alarm and they both fled. About five minutes later, an unmarked police car with two white plain clothes cops pulled up and parked adjacent to the street box. The cop sitting in the passenger seat made a hand gesture toward the street box, looked directly at me and said, "Did you pull that alarm nigger?"

WHY POLICE ABOLITION

Several years ago, while presenting a paper at the American Society of Criminology's annual conference, I decided to share the news that I was preparing to write my next book on dismantling American policing. The reactions were a mixture of bewilderment and intellectual hostility. "Why" became a question I would hear repeatedly over the next several years, primarily within white spaces in the academy. I heard it from criminal justice faculty, criminal justice students, and all types of criminal justice practitioners alike. "Why" conduct research on the inconceivably taboo criminal justice topic of police abolition. Many white colleagues cautioned me that exploring this topic would be the "kiss of death" for my criminal justice program and that it would hurt my credibility with policing agencies, which would

1

negatively impact student recruitment and retention, since the overwhelming majority of criminal justice majors, specifically those that have an interest in policing careers, are primarily white, male, and politically conservative. I explained that this was not a research project. I explained that I do not distinguish conducting research from living a Black life. You see, this was an ongoing dialogue with my people, Black people. An evolving organic critical autoethnography, which took place over the course of nearly fifty years of my life. "How do we get policing out of our lives" is just one of many dialogues of resistance that take place within the space of the Black radical tradition in America. But the academies' racial obtuseness was steadfast. This reminded me of the haunting words of E. Franklin Frazier (1962) in *The Failure of the Negro Intellectual*, which describes the intellectual coffin where many Black scholars are forced to be buried alive, within the academy:

> All of this only tends to underline the fact that educated Negroes or Negro intellectuals have failed to achieve any intellectual freedom. In fact, with the few exceptions of literary men, it appears that the Negro intellectual is unconscious of the extent to which his thinking is restricted to sterile repetition of the safe and conventional ideas current in American society. This is attributable in part, of course, to the conditions under which an educated and intellectual class emerged in the American society. This class emerged as the result of white American philanthropy. Although the situation has changed and the Negro intellectuals are supported through other means, they are still largely dependent upon the white community. There is no basis of economic support for them within the Negro community. And where there is economic support within the Negro community it demands conformity to conservative and conventional ideas. (pp. 26–36)

According to D. Soyini Madison (2012) in *Critical Ethnography: Methods, Ethics, and Performance*, critical ethnography begins with an ethical responsibility to address processes of unfairness and/or injustice within a particular lived domain (p. 5). I believe this is done by examining the voices and stories of those who have been systemically *Othered*. What my white academic colleagues could not or would not understand is that I have always written as an *Other* and for an *Other* (Gaskew & Thompson, 2020c). Within this framework, there is an obligation to resist white domestication; to search beneath surface appearances in order to expose obscure constructs of white power and control; and to move from what is to what could be. I have a metaphysical duty to emancipate knowledge. An obligation to move from policing to abolishing policing. Arguably, there has not been a greater systemic injustice applied to any people in America, more than how policing and its long history of political violence against the Black diaspora, in its attempt to subjugate and colonize. Hence, there is an unquestionable obligation to challenge the policing narrative, resist police violence, and expose policing's inherent cultural weakness and flaws, in a collective effort to force this institution to dismantle. My commitment to using my knowledge and skills in the service of improving the human condition, improving the Pan-Afrikan condition, is a reflection of *ma'at*, my cosmic link to Afrikan minds, bodies, and spirits. I will explore *ma'at* in much greater detail later in the book. I am always moving from my Afrikan unconsciousness to my Afrikan consciousness.

With my intellectual freedom fully intact, I did exactly what a Black male intellectual or a *sesh* should do when faced with an abundance of white privilege and white fragility. I decided to teach a criminal justice class on police abolition. As I was preparing the syllabus, I called dozens of criminal justice program directors across the country, inquiring whether they had ever offered a course on police abolition. Although a few indicated they had breached the topic of abolition, it was only within the context of prison abolition, never police abolition. After eighteen months of planning, in the spring 2019 academic term, I taught a first-of-its-kind undergraduate University of Pittsburgh criminal justice course entitled *ADMJ 1449: Special Topics—Abolishing the Police*. The course description is as follows (Gaskew, 2019):

> This course will explore the reality of police abolition in America. This course will introduce students into building collaborative relationships with grassroots organizations from Oakland, California, Washington, DC, Minneapolis, Minnesota, and Chicago, Illinois who focus their efforts on the development of new community-controlled alternatives to policing in America. (p. 1)

The required readings list was extensive, and included Richard Delgado and Jean Stefancic's *Critical Race Theory: An Introduction*, Peter Gelderloos's *How Nonviolence Protects the State*, and various materials from the *Anti Police-Terror Project, Baltimore Bloc, Black Lives Matter-Chicago, Black Lives Matter-DC, Black Youth Project 100, Chicago Alliance Against Racial Repression, Critical Resistance, A World Without Police, Lamont Lilly, MPD150, Stop Police Terror Project DC, The Abolitionist*, and the *Movement for Black Lives* (Gaskew, 2019, pp. 1–2). The course was populated by all undergraduate criminal justice majors, who provided excellent quantitative student evaluations. However, two qualitative student evaluative comments stood out (University of Pittsburgh, 2019). The first comment read:

> I never realized there were so many groups that wanted to abolish the police. I think it is a good class for CJ and other majors to take. Very interesting and gets people to think a different way. (p. 4)

The second student's comment read:

> I think this class is even more valuable because not many professors that are
> CJ professionals would teach a class like this, and most people try to mask the
> profession under the blue line. (p. 4)

These two anonymous student evaluative comments, the only qualitative
comments, both from criminal justice majors, speak volumes for themselves.
However, one of the most uncomfortable aspects of the course were our
class discussions on the language of revolution. That is, I discovered that the
majority of the white criminal justice majors in the course were very uneasy
with the term *revolution*, especially if it was coupled with the terms *Black
Power* or *Black armed resistance*. The overwhelming majority of the Black
criminal justice majors were clearly more comfortable with the realities of
"why" the terms were applicable to police abolition. I introduced two guest
speakers within the course curriculum—one a nationally known Black activ-
ist/revolutionary and the other, the head of a national police abolition organization—and both used these terms interchangeably during their lectures. The
entire experience of the course, again, probably the first-of-its-kind within the
academic discipline of criminal justice, provided me with an abundance of
field notes and maybe some additional future articles; however, it clearly left
me with a much larger frame of inquiry: How do you speak the language of
revolution today, as it relates to the dismantling of American policing?

THE LANGUAGE OF REVOLUTION

How is the construct of revolution operationalized within many abolitionist
movements today? As noted earlier, organized abolitionist movements today
are a strange mixture of pathological pacifists and intellectual capitalists,
who feed off the deaths of the Black male bodies at the hands of state violence. Thus, in order to speak the language of revolution through the voices
of the Black radical tradition, it's invaluable to understand how the concept
of revolution has been packaged for liberal consumption. *A World Without
Police* (2019), a collective of organizers from across the United States and
internationally, who work to connect people struggling against the everyday
violence of the police, states:

> We believe police violence and exploitation cannot be ended through reforms
> (better trained, better monitored, more friendly cops) but only with the total abo-
> lition of the police as an institution. As we explain, this is because police forces
> maintain the inequalities of capitalist society and will continue to be violent

and racist as long as they exist. At the same time, we know police abolition is only possible as part of a broader revolutionary project to abolish the state in its entirety, along with capitalism, white supremacy and patriarchy. The struggle against the police cannot be divided from the broader movement or treated as a single-issue campaign. This is because "the police" is more than just a group of men and women who wear badges: it is also a historical project of division, upholding a social order where the lives of Black, POC, poor, queer and trans people's lives are forfeit. If we only disband police departments, their role could be replaced by non-uniformed security guards, white supremacist militias and patriarchal family networks without fundamentally transforming our social relations. A world without police—not simply as police exist now, but as a form of division—requires revolution. (para. 2–4)

MPD150 (2019a), a police abolitionist organization based out of Minneapolis, suggests that police reform is an inherent impossibility in America:

The police were established to protect the interests of the wealthy and racialized violence has always been a part of that mission. The police cannot be reformed away from their core function. The police criminalize dark skin and poverty, channeling millions of people into the prison system, depriving them of voting and employment rights and thereby preserve privileged access to housing, jobs, land, credit and education for whites. (para. 2–4)

The *Anti Police-Terror Project* (2019a), an Oakland based, Black-led, intergenerational coalition that works toward police abolition, notes:

APTP has never subscribed to the belief that policing in America can be fixed. The system is not broken and thus cannot be made to right itself. Born of the slave trade, policing in America was then—and is now—about the catching, killing and incarcerating of Black and Indigenous bodies. We are an abolitionist organization committed to interrupting and rapidly responding to state violence, radically transforming the way in which we as a society define public safety and develop new practices to implement community security that are not rooted in race-based capitalism, white supremacy, patriarchy, racism, violence, rape and murder. (para. 1–9)

Critical Resistance (2019a), one of the first abolitionist organizations in the America, with chapters in Los Angeles, New York City, Oakland, and Portland, noted the following during an interview with communications director Mohamed Shehk (Shiffer, 2017):

We work to abolish policing, imprisonment, and the rest of the prison industrial complex because we believe that they are fundamentally violent and racist. Our work as abolitionists is not to improve a war machine built to target Black and

Brown people, but to chip away and disempower policing and imprisonment so that they have less power to function, with the ultimate goal of shrinking them into nonexistence.

After reading dozens of bold and informative abolitionist vision statements that openly reject state violence, many of whom are based on the ideological and political beliefs of historic Black radicals, and the millions of dollars pouring into movements such as BLM, you have to ask yourself why hasn't the pendulum of police abolition moved so much as an inch toward reality? I would humbly offer, many of the white liberals who fund, lead, and supply the personnel that fill these organizations with fresh warm bodies, notwithstanding the fact that most liberals do not want an America without the police, primarily because the human capital made from dead Black men at the hands of policing violence is much more profitable than ever imagined—they do not understand the *ritual* of revolution. They cannot understand the *ritual* of revolution. They have never performed the *ritual* of revolution. They have never lived or experienced the *ritual* of revolution. And just to be very clear, based on dozens of interviews with abolitionist's movements across the country, staffed and led by Black groups, who identify under a wide spectrum of political and ideological affiliations, they share the hypnotic fear and paranoid rejection of the *ritual* of revolution. To them, it is much easier and much more profitable to stand in the middle of the street, scream at the police, and be shot directly in the face by a rubber bullet. And more ominously, to convince millions of others to do the same, day after day, year after year, with no tangible results to show. Rather than to commit to use every conceivable tactic available in the ritual of revolution, to liberate themselves and others from state violence. Although there are outlier individuals and groups, abolitionist organizations, including BLM, are viewed as systemically weak, and thus are easily infiltrated through counterinsurgency operations by the police, who routinely approve of their movement leadership. Although publically ridiculed by the policing culture, they are embraced internally because "twitter revolutionaries" generate hundreds of millions of dollars in overtime compensation. As I describe later in the book, abolitionist organizations can play a role in communicating data and material information that can be helpful in disputing the national policing narrative, but this is largely overshadowed by their lack of actionable results and pathological pacifism.

Only the *ritual* of revolution can dismantle the institution of policing in America. Sobunfu Somé (2000, p. 21) in *The Spirit of Intimacy: Ancient African Teachings in the Ways of Relationships* defines a *ritual* as a cosmological open-ended performance that summons our ancestral spirits to participate in human affairs. Rituals open a sacred indigenous space, vetted in the Kemetic virtues of truth, justice, balance, harmony, order, righteousness, and reciprocity, for our ancestors, our indigenous collective energy, to present themselves in our consciousness. Rituals unify the cosmic bond that exist between the past and the present. Rituals are the most indigenous platform for binding communities through the dimensions of time and space. Malidoma Patrice Somé (1998, p. 141) in *The Healing Wisdom of Africa: Finding Life Purpose through Nature, Ritual, and Community* describes the two dialectic phases and the four synergized steps in the ritual process: planned and unplanned; preparing the ritual space, invocation, healing, and closing. Planning the ritual involves creating the physical and spiritual space in our consciousness to connect with our ancestral energy. The unplanned phase of the ritual is the uncontrollable interaction between the physical and spiritual worlds. As Somé (1998, p. 142) points out, "It is like a journey. Before you get started, you own the journey. After you start, the journey owns you." The steps in the ritual process are just as nuanced. First, we must possess the indigenous ability to create a space where our ancestors are welcome. The ritual space should be representative of the spirit of *ma'at* and the five elements (water, fire, earth, nature, and mineral). Second, we must possess the cosmic ability to connect and communicate with our ancestors through many forms of consciousness. An "open mind" created through the prism of meditation, for example, serves as the gateway to various forms of consciousness, allowing us to surrender ourselves to our ancestral energy. Third, we enter the healing part of the process, arguably the key to the entire ritual. Somé (1998, p. 154) stresses that "if nothing happens here, then the ritual did not happen." Healing is described as a state of deep awareness beyond self-consciousness, which many times invokes a genuine uncontrollable emotional energy, followed by a period of calmness and reflection. Finally, closing the ritual process involves an outpouring of gratitude for the presence of our ancestors' energy and the fulfillment of their purpose. It is just as important to release the spirit of our ancestors as it is to call for their presence.

Kaba Kamene (2019) in *Spirituality Before Religions: Spirituality is Unseen Science . . . Science is Seen Spirituality* argues that the ritual process is part of the Kemetic energy that lives deep inside the indigenous Black soul. Communicating with our ancestors is part of the Pan-Afrikan cultural DNA. Rituals have been part of the culture of the Black diaspora since the existence of humankind, and this includes rituals of war (Somé, 2000). Rituals of resistance, self-defense, and liberation will always be Afrikan phenomena. In fact, the Black revolution of the 1960s is a direct extension of Afrikan wars of liberation, which includes the Haitian Revolution and Bois Caïman. The ritual of revolution has always been a species of warfare within the Black diaspora. My voice is echoed in Vincent Brown's (2020) *Tacky's Revolt: The Story of an Atlantic Slave War*, Cedric Robinson's (1983) *Black Marxism:*

The Making of the Black Radical Tradition, and Julius Scott's (2018) *The Common Wind: Afro-American Currents in the Age of the Haitian Revolution*.

Hence, understanding that revolution is an indigenous metaphysical ritual, shaped by countless generations of Black resistance to global oppression, it's much easier to see how white liberals, their colonized Black allies, and the abolitionist movements they lead and fund will only support the platform of reform and can never embrace revolution. As such, nothing short of the ritual of revolution will be required to dismantle policing in America. Anyone who tells you differently is profiting from white supremacy, is colonized, or simply fears the inevitable fall of the empire. There is no middle ground. Every single time I hear someone beg, preach, or cry for reform efforts after an incident of systemic police violence, I am reminded of what an incarcerated Black revolutionary once told me: "Either try to dismantle policing, or shut the fuck up." The Black Liberation Army (1971) argued that the rejection of a reformist platform runs much deeper than some theoretical debate on tactics, because reformism is a complete rejection of revolution, adding "Reformism is a function of ignorance of the dynamics of Black liberation."

I will argue throughout this book that the ritual of revolution is required to dismantle a system of oppression like policing. I will argue that this ritual is found in the voices of the Black radical tradition. A ritual based on Black consciousness. A ritual based on Black resistance. A ritual based on Black organization. A ritual based on Black action. A ritual of revolution that speaks the language of police abolition. As Fred Hampton (1969c) noted, "Theory's cool, but theory with no practice ain't shit." Clearly, this ritual of revolution has been conceived within the ancestral womb of the Black Power Movement of the 1960s.

According to Kwame Ture (2003, pp. 520–563) in his autobiography, *Ready for Revolution: The Life and Struggles of Stokely Carmichael (Kwame Ture)*, revolution is Black power and Black power is revolution. It speaks the political and cultural core of truth and justice. Black people are not afraid to speak and practice truths that will hurt the psyche of whiteness. Ture (2003) argued that Black power is not one single act, not one single battle on a single front, but a whole epoch of intensified conflicts, a long series of battles on all fronts, that is, battles around all the problems of economics, politics, and race that make up what we know as white supremacy. He challenged the Black diaspora to see revolution as more than an adjective or a noun; revolution as a dynamic, complicated, and organic process; revolution as anti-liberalism. Revolution sets the tone and language for liberal outrage. Revolution speaks the language of political and cultural power, consciously and publicly freeing ourselves from the heritage of white supremacy, decolonizing our Black souls and Black bodies. Revolution is not new to the Pan-Afrikan diaspora. It is a conversation we've had since our ancestors arrived in chains. This conversation has never stopped. Revolution is discussed inside barbershops and university lecture halls. Revolution is discussed in military bases, police departments, prisons, and daycare centers. The ideological and metaphysical forces of revolution are in the Black radical cultural and political DNA. Revolution is what I saw, heard, tasted, and breathed growing up as a child of the Black Power Movement in Chicago. Revolution lives in our birth and death cycle. Revolution is all we know.

The Black Liberation Army (1971) argues that revolution is not only one of the most critical actions the Black diaspora must take in its quest for liberation. The BLA argues that because of the unique *advanced oppression* produced by America's version of white supremacy on Black lives, the Black revolution in America will serve as the vanguard movement of all revolutions. The Black Liberation Army (1971) notes:

> We understand the process of revolution. For Black people here in North America, our struggle is not only unique, but it is the most sophisticated and advanced oppression of a racial national minority in the world... [Revolution] will find its highest development as a result of us. (p. 4)

You see, revolution dictates that Black people always learn more from our enemies than from our allies. Revolution pushes back on assimilation, which has always been an element of cultural and political suicide. Revolution is about *power*. The power to affirm Black humanity. The power to defend the dignity, integrity, and institutions of Black culture. The power to collectively organize the political and economic means to empower Black communities. Black power is about pride, self-respect, and autonomy. The two primary questions become how to self-define the revolution against the political, economic, or cultural forces behind policing and what kinds of changes are required to alter the power relationship between policing and the Pan-Afrikan experience in America.

How can Black communities dismantle the institution of policing when these same Black communities do not believe they control the resources that provide the life blood of their Black resistance? White power sustains policing in Black communities, by arming the policing culture with a variety of weapons of oppression. Black communities feel powerless to fight them back. The ritual of revolution shifts this narrative. Black power shifts the universe of white supremacy. Black power arms the Black diaspora with Black powder. Revolution dismantles the existing relationship between policing and Black communities in America. The ritual of revolution requires that everything that Black people were ever told or taught about policing from their white allies must be challenged. Revolution requires creative ways for Black communities to take back our lives from policing. The ritual of revolution requires a protracted and organized conflict against the institution of policing.

Ture (1971) noted in *From Black Power to Pan-Africanism* that revolutionary ideology must be based on the philosophy of dialectics, that is, the philosophy of opposites. Revolution must be scientific. It must be consistent. It must be based on a thorough and complete analysis of history. There is no compromise in revolution. Revolution knows no compromise. Revolutionary ideology must dictate that two objects cannot occupy the same space at the same time. You can't have American policing and Black liberation in America at the same time. Revolution mandates a violent clash, and only one will win. Ture (1971) described the Vietnamese as one of the best examples of a revolutionary people, who during the American invasion lived under the creed, "either we will win, or we will die." They clearly understood that they were fighting a system that was diametrically opposed to their own liberation and knew that they either drove the United States out of their lives or face death. They handily defeated the United States. Ture (1971) believed that Afrikans in America must use the same revolutionary process for their own liberation. This same revolutionary process must be used to abolish policing from the lives of the Black diaspora in America.

According to El Hajj Malik El Shabazz (1964), in his speech "The Black Revolution," revolution always centered on defending the land from systems of oppression:

> Revolution is always based on land. Revolution is never based on begging somebody for an integrated cup of coffee. Revolutions are never fought by turning the other cheek. Revolutions are never based upon love-your-enemy and pray-for-those-who-despitefully-use-you. And revolutions are never waged singing "We Shall Overcome." Revolutions are based on bloodshed. Revolutions are never compromising. Revolutions are never based upon negotiations. Revolutions are never based upon any kind of tokenism whatsoever. Revolutions are never even based upon that which is begging a corrupt society or a corrupt system to accept us into it. Revolutions overturn systems. And there is no system on this earth which has proven itself more corrupt, more criminal, than this system [America]. (para. 19)

Understand that within the Black diaspora, centered on our cosmological *Ari*, the people and the land are one collective within the universe. As the aboriginals, the Black diaspora is formed from the five elements: *fire, water, earth, mineral,* and *nature* (Somé, 1998). The Black diaspora is the land. The Black diaspora suffers or flourishes, as a direct reflection of the land. Thus, revolution is always based on the land. As such, as the vanguards of the planet, the Black diaspora is morally obligated under *ma'at* to defend the land. To defend the community. To defend the diaspora. Understanding that self-defense is a universal mandate of all living being, the Black diaspora will defend itself from all systems of oppression that threaten the land. Thus, the ritual of revolution is always centered on overturning systems of oppression.

According to Fred Hampton (1969a), in his speech "Power Anywhere Where There's People," revolution is the cure for America's ills, but it requires truth:

> There's three basic things that you got to do anytime you intend to have yourself a successful revolution. A lot of people get the word revolution mixed up and they think revolution's a bad word. Revolution is nothing but like having a sore on your body and then you put something on that sore to cure that infection. And I'm telling you that we're living in an infectious society right now. I'm telling you that we're living in a sick society. And anybody that endorses integrating into this sick society before it cleaned up is a man who's committing a crime against the people. (para.1–10)

The ritual of revolution is not only about destruction. Revolutionary violence is centered on building and creating. Revolution is about innovation: to dismantle in order to build. Dismantling is an inevitable consequence of building. Revolution requires that all systems of oppression must be dismantled in order for new systems to be built. Revolution is about systemic dismantling and systemic creation. The ritual of revolution is about systemically dismantling American policing. Revolution is about systemically building systems that are diametrically opposed to white supremacy. Revolution is about systemically creating viable alternatives to American policing. The ritual of revolution is about educating the Black diaspora in America on the tactics of violence and nonviolence. Revolution is about acquiring knowledge of Pan-Afrikanism. Revolution is about evolving Pan-Afrikanism and organizing police abolitionism into a mass movement. According to Balagoon (2019):

> Make no mistake, without a mass movement there is no revolution. A mass movement, on the other hand, can organize the people and set the conditions for the building of real peoples armies, which will not only have the power to carry on protracted war but will build the forces strong enough to sweep the government and ruling class out of power. No individual can carry out a revolution, only organization. (p. 229)

The Black Liberation Army (1971) added:

> Unless the movement cultivates its capacity to fight the enemy on all fronts, no front will secure any real victories. Our oppressor maintains armed organs of

violence for the enforcement of his rules. We as a movement will be unable to fight in the future if we do not develop the capacity for revolutionary violence in the present. But revolutionary violence is not an alternative to mass movement and organization, it is complementary to mass struggle, it is another front in the total liberation process. (p. 18)

According to Hampton (1969a) revolution is the culmination of community empowerment:

We ain't gonna fight no reactionary pigs who run up and down the street being reactionary; we're gonna organize and dedicate ourselves to revolutionary political power and teach ourselves the specific needs of resisting the power structure, arm ourselves, and we're gonna fight reactionary pigs with international proletarian revolution. That's what it has to be. The people have to have the power: it belongs to the people. (para.1–10)

Having a physical, psychological, and spiritual oneness with Pan-Afrikanism is a requirement for the ritual of revolution. Ture (1971) believed white supremacy was the same in apartheid South Africa as it was in Jim Crow Mississippi. The ritual of revolution teaches us that the slave patrols in the Caribbean in 1661 are no different than those in New York City in 2020. From breeding farms to stop and frisk, they are the same—the same states, the same interests, the same schemes, and the same policing. Thus, they both require the same ideological understanding of Pan-Afrikanism and of revolution. The problems of Afrika are the problems of Afrikans in America: we are both landless, victims of capitalism, victims of racism, and victims of policing. According to Ture (1971):

Many people when they try to analyze the problems of the Afrikan in America, calls it a problem peculiar to America. They take the history back to the Afrikans when they came to America. That's absurd. The problem didn't start in America. The problem started in Afrika when the first white man came to rape us of our continent and of our people. That's where the problem started. That's the roots of the problem. The first white boy that came there and tried to get us had to fight. That's where the problem started. America is only an extension of the war. A tangent, if you will. But the problem didn't start in America. It started in Afrika. We fought in Afrika, we fought in the slave ships, we fought in America, we fought during slavery, we fought after slavery, we've been fighting, and we continue to fight because it's only an extended war. (para. 1–20)

Thus, the ritual of revolution used for dismantling the institution of American policing, today's slave patrols, is a 340-year ongoing and uninterrupted odyssey of self-consciousness, self-determinism, and self-defense. The revolution against policing has never stopped. It has only gone through a period of *evolution* and *involution* (Kamene, 2019, p. 9). According to James Boggs and Grace Lee Boggs (1974, pp. 13–23), in *Revolution and Evolution in the Twentieth Century*, the relationship between revolutionary ideas and revolutionary practice must lead to revolutionary action. Theory and practice must be connected to action. Theory, practice, and action for dismantling the institution of policing are generated from reflection and past experiences. Therefore, any new perspective on the ritual of revolution, especially one centered on dismantling policing, can be found within the birth canal of the Black Power Movement of the 1960s.

Since police abolition relies on the ritual of revolution, we must ask ourselves, what did the Black Power Movement teach us about dismantling the institution of American policing? The signature of Black studies (Karenga, 2010) is clear on these facts: the Black radical tradition, by way of the BPP, the RNA, and the BLA, led the way. Everything we know about police abolition today has been inherited from the DNA of this Black radical tradition. However, given their historic significance, we must be critical and ask, are the Black movements today, such as the McDonaldization of BLM across the nation, actually practicing capitalism? Are they applying any of the lessons taught by their radical Black revolutionary ancestors? I realize that's probably a conversation for a different book, but it's very important that we clearly understand how the ritual of revolution must be applied to dismantling policing. Boggs & Boggs (1974) state that to understand what a revolution is, we must be very clear about what a revolution is not:

> A revolution is not the same as a *rebellion* or an *insurrection* or a *revolt* or a *coup d'état*. A *rebellion* is an attack upon existing authority by members of an oppressed group with no intention on the part of the rebels to take state power. It is usually spontaneous. An *insurrection* is a concentrated attack upon existing authority by members of an oppressed group, usually with the intention of taking power, if only temporarily, during the course of revolutionary struggles or at the culmination of a process of revolutionary struggle. A *revolt* is an organized attempt to seize power, usually by a section of the armed forces, without prior organization of the masses in struggle and without any clear set of social objectives. A *coup d'état* is the successful overthrow of existing authority in one audacious stroke, usually by a section of the armed forces. All these are single events, limited in time as well as in target and objective. (pp. 13–24)

Historically, surely we can agree that discussing a revolt or a coup d'état in America is pointless, since it requires a separate armed wing of state white supremacy to turn against the current armed wing of state white supremacy, with the goal of creating a new armed wing of state white supremacy. Although theoretically a possibility, the institution of American policing stays intact, in one form or the other. That leaves rebellions and insurrections. Boggs & Boggs (1974) argue that rebellions and insurrections may take place in the course of revolutionary struggle, but they do not constitute revolution. The recent rebellion to reform, defund, and abolish American policing after the murder of George Floyd, largely reflected in nonviolent protests, demonstrations, rallies, hashtag activism, and parades—a collective of police and communities marching together—across the nation, has resulted in one of the largest accumulations of police overtime in American history. In just fourteen days, New York City Police Department (NYPD) officers took home a staggering $115 million in overtime pay (Nguyen, 2020). I'm confident that the New York City Police Pension Fund (2020) would gladly send each and every protestor in NYC a personalized thank you card. By the end of this protest cycle, pathological pacifism will have rewarded the institution of policing in America, some of their highest yearly earnings to record, with not one single tangible outcome that will end the state-authorized execution of the next George Floyd.

During some of my discussions with abolitionist organizations, social justice groups, and activists who were advocating for the abolishment of policing, they all framed their actions—demonstrations, rallies, and protests—as "revolutionary in spirit." What is evidently clear is that there is no willingness to engage in revolution. Even though activists use the rhetoric of revolution, they are solidly much more into building consensus for police reform and obtaining incremental changes within the policing narrative. There is no urgency to obtain power to govern, just a desire for intersectional group status. Nobody can dispute the popularity of young activists, with millions of followers on various social media platforms. According to Goldmacher (2020), racial justice and Black-led advocacy groups, including the NAACP Legal Defense and Educational Fund and the Black Lives Matter Global Network, received tens of millions of dollars in donations since the death of George Floyd, with significant funding originating from corporate America. In fact, big corporations such as the Warner Brothers Music Group and the Sony Music Group pledged $100 million each.

But for Kwame Ture (1967a,b,c,d, 1972, 1973) revolution is neither *idealistic*, nor *romantic*, nor *escapist*. Revolution is not about money. Revolution is not about status. Revolution is about organization. Revolution is about power. Revolutionary thinking begins with a series of illuminations. A thinking that has purpose. A thinking that is about the masses. A revolution is not just for the purpose of correcting past injustices against Black people in America. A revolution involves a projection of a Pan-Afrikan future. It begins with projecting the notion of a liberated Black experience. A Black experience that uses revolutionary creativity, revolutionary consciousness, and a sense of revolutionary political and cultural ownership. A Pan-Afrikan conscious struggle. That is, a struggle governed by Pan-Afrikan conscious values, Pan-Afrikan conscious goals, Pan-Afrikan conscious programs, and Pan-Afrikan conscious people is required. Within this collective definition of the ritual of revolution, we find the evolution of CRT.

THE LANGUAGE OF POLICE ABOLITION

Critical race theory (CRT), the transformational vision of Derrick Bell (1992a), was initially introduced to the Black masses in the early 1970s, places racism and the actionable poison of white supremacy as a permanent component of the construct behind the enslavement of millions of Earth's first humans, and the creation of the settler colony, the United States (Bell, 1984, 1987, 1988, 1990). CRT advocates that white supremacy and its product, racism, is a permanent part of all American institutions (Bell, 1984, 1987, 1988, 1990). The truth behind the permanence of racism, in what Bell (1992b) described as *real racism*, cannot be swayed by white liberal pipe dreams and fantasies of equity and justice that have been served up like raw meat to the Black masses in America to digest since 1619.

According to Richard Delgado and Jean Stefancic (2017, pp. 3–155), in *Critical Race Theory: An Introduction*, CRT examines the relationship between race, racism, and power. CRT questions the very foundations of the liberal order in America, including equality theory, legal reasoning, enlightenment rationalism, and all so-called neutral principles of constitutional law. Using the voices and storytelling of Black people, CRT questions the very foundation of whiteness. More importantly, CRT questions the reasoning and rationale of every theory that originated from whiteness: Marx, Freud, Engels, Merton, Durkheim, Goffman, Parsons, Mead, Merton, Simmel, Spencer, Webber, The Chicago School, and so on. Although Derrick Bell is considered the intellectual father of CRT within the applied practice of law, it has rapidly spread far beyond him and any single discipline and mantra. Unlike some academic disciplines, CRT embodies the Black radical tradition and embraces a revolutionary dimension. As a critical race theorist, my goal is not only to expose the permanence of white supremacy within the systemic institution of policing and examine an applied methodology to dismantle the institution of policing from the ground up but also to provide an aboriginally based foundation of how we can evolve our understanding of justice.

Delgado & Stefancic (2017, pp. 8–11) argue that CRT sits on several basic tenets. First, that white supremacy and its by-product racism are ordinary and not aberrational. That white supremacy and racism is a normal phenomenon, a normal science, the usual way society does business, and the common. I would add here that white supremacy and racism is demonstrated in the everyday lived experiences of every Black person in America, including within their inevitable contacts with policing. Second, most Black people would agree that our system of white supremacy and racism serves important purposes, both psychic and material, for the innocence of whiteness. White supremacy's "ordinariness" is difficult to dismantle because it is hidden in the womb of white liberalism (more on this throughout the chapter), advancing the interests of white elites, the white middle class, and poor whites. Policing lives within and is culturally protected by this womb. There are no political or economic incentives for whites, any white person in America, to eradicate white supremacy. As I will argue throughout this book, police abolition is a pipedream if it depends on white American action. The third and fourth themes of CRT hold that race, races, and racialization are psycho-social constructs and by-products of macro thought and relations. Policing does not exist because of its inevitable collision with Black lives. It exists because it serves to validate the existence of white power and its psychic violence. The fifth and sixth themes hold that each person behind the construct of race has their own origins and ever-evolving history and that CRT examines the concerns of locating the unique voice of oppression in America. Melanin is a rainbow of Blackness. This *rainbow* has many voices to be heard and stories to tell regarding the oppressive nature of policing in America. I would argue that two central themes must be explored when applying CRT to police abolition: Is the Black experience with policing in America the voice and stories of global oppression? Is the Black liberation from policing in America the solution to the global liberation of oppression?

As noted by almost every critical race theorist, white liberalism serves to validate systemic white superiority and Black inferiority. For critical race scholars like myself, it's disgustingly laughable that white liberalism is being used as the framework for solving white supremacy and America's racial problems in policing. White liberals benefit from white supremacy. White liberals benefit from policing. White liberals adopt the tenets of color blindness and neutral principles of policing. Color blindness of any form is detrimental to Black liberation and the dismantling of policing institutions. White supremacy is embedded in the thought processes and cultural language of policing in America. The "ordinary business" of policing is consumed by the warped rituals, routines, and tactics of psychic violence. CRT argues that stop and frisk, racial profiling, and excessive force are specifically designed to keep Black people in America in a subordinate metaphysical state of mind. CRT argues that revolutionary actions within the Black radical tradition will be required to dismantle and abolish policing in America.

Delgado & Stefancic (2017, pp. 77–85) also point out how CRT challenges the notion of how we are taught about the paradigm of race. That is, the conception that race in the United States consists, either exclusively or primarily, of only two constituent socially constructed racial groups: the Black and the white. In addition, the paradigm dictates that all other ethnic identities and groups in America are only understood through the Black-white binary lens. Non-Black oppressed groups (Latinx, First Nation, etc.) in the United States must compare their treatment to that of the Black diaspora in America, in order to redress their own grievances. This practice of white supremacy weakens solidarity, reduces opportunities for coalition, deprives a group of the benefits of the *Others* experiences, makes it excessively dependent on the approval of the white establishment, and sets it up for ultimate disappointment (pp. 77–85). The history of Black, Latinx, Asian, and First Nation people in the Unites States shows that while one group is trying to gain political and cultural power, another is often losing it. CRT argues that white people often cast Black people against all other ethnic groups, at the detriment of each group. This is how white supremacy operates within a colonization paradigm. In addition to pitting Afrikans in America against other ethnic groups, binary thinking induces oppressed groups to identify with whites in an exaggerated fashion at the expense of other groups. For example, in California Asians sought to be declared "white" to attend schools for whites; Mexican Americans pursued "other white" policies (League of United Latin American Citizens) insisting that society treat Latinx as white (pp. 77–85).

The CRT assessment of the Black-white binary is clearly applied within the institution of policing in America. You do not have to look any further than the police-generated data warehouses of the Uniform Crime Report (UCR), the National Incident-Based Reporting System (NIBRS), and the National Crime Victimization Survey (NCVS). Each was designed to solidify the Black-white binary, manufacturing skewed data and developing a system to categorize this skewed data into two constituent socially constructed racial groups: Black and white. The significance of data generated on any other ethnic identity category used by these data warehouses is only understood through the Black-white binary lens. One of the most blatant examples of this binary lens can be found in how the Latinx population in America has been statistically categorized within these data sets. Since the creation of the UCR in 1929, all data (police activity) generated on Latinx people in the United States has been classified into the racial category of "white." This is not only another example of the egregious ethical behavior of the FBI but further establishes the depth by which the Black-white binary in policing is used to manufacture invisible communities, where people, and in this example Latinx communities and Latinx people, are forced to solidify their existence by only comparing their treatment to that of the Black diaspora. Policing *uses* the

Latinx population to systemically inflate "white" arrest data, which has had policy ramifications that we will never completely understand. The institution of policing has used police generated data on Latinx populations to *white-wash* their experiences, making these communities excessively dependent on the approval of the white establishment, setting them up the Latinx people for the ultimate disappointment and betrayal. As we can now see, the FBI has established a separate ethnic category for the Latinx population in their crime data bases, willingly exploiting the Latinx crime and arrest data, in order to weaponize immigration legislation against their culture, community, and contributions to America. I will further discuss the UCR, NIBRS, and NCVS later in the book.

We must remember that Black-white binary thinking in policing can also cause Black people in America to go along with a reoccurring ploy in which whites, especially liberal whites, choose usually a small, tough-on-crime, blue-lives-matter, nonthreatening group of Blacks—many working within the criminal justice field—to serve as examples of "good Blacks" and the overseers of the *other*—"the bad Blacks." Black people in America that fall into this trap hope to gain status, while whites can tell themselves that they are not racists because they have employed a certain number of suitably grateful Blacks as police chiefs, prosecutors, wardens, and judges. This is the perfect model that explains the selection and recruitment of Blacks into policing. Whites choose the most non-threatening Black people to employ in policing—ones they know will reproduce colonial white supremacist results. I will discuss this phenomenon at great lengths in chapter 5.

Speaking the language of CRT provides us the unique teaching power to challenge our own preconceptions, privileges, and standpoints from which we, as Afrikans in America, reason on the issue of policing. It teaches Afrikans in America to never question the basis of how we see our existence in America. To never acknowledge that white supremacy demands that we are to be colonized and programmed to see and hear the world through a set of white eyes and white ears. To lose our true aboriginal nature and our universal instinct of self-preservation. CRT teaches us to shift the unconscious to conscious. It teaches us that the first step in fighting white supremacy is to understand that it is the written and spoken language of the American culture (Welsing, 1992). Imagine, what the Black experience in America and globally would be like if we all spoke the language of dismantling systems of oppression.

Under my new paradigm, CRT holds an intellectual mirror to whiteness and conducts a critical analysis of the white race and its inherent relationship with policing. A new generation of Black criminal justice scholars must place whiteness under a critical lens and examine the construction of how policing has become an instrument of white liberal identity politics. Policing is whiteness. Policing is white ethno-nationalism. Thus, policing assigns itself with white myths. Policing assigns itself with innocence or goodness. Policing assigns itself as normal. Policing assigns itself as the standard. Policing has become part of America's pop-culture phenomenon, reinforcing the myth of white superiority and Black inferiority, one tweet at a time. As noted later in this book, the Barbados Slave Code of 1661 set the tone of how policing would be constructed in America. It gave policing a legal mantra, equipping an armed militia to enforce, protect, and colonize the concept of whiteness. CRT provides the lens to see whiteness, not only as an assigned value but as a value that shifts and is malleable under the worldview of American policing (Delgado & Stefancic, 2017, p. 89; Gaskew, 2020a). Let's not forget that white privilege refers to the myriad of assigned social advantages, benefits, and courtesies that come with whiteness (p. 89). Policing is the construct that upholds, enforces, and synergizes white privilege and white power in America.

THE EVOLUTION OF CRITICAL RACE THEORY INTO POLICING ABOLITION

Police violence is a leading cause of death for young Black men in the United States. Over their life course, about 1 in every 1,000 Black men can expect to be killed by the police (Edwards, Lee, & Esposito, 2019; Fatal Encounters, 2019). In fact, according to Mark Hoekstra and Carly Sloan (2020) in *Does Race Matter for Police Use of Force? Evidence from 911 Calls*, while white and Black police officers use gun force at similar rates in white and racially mixed neighborhoods, white police officers are five times as likely to use gun force in predominantly Black neighborhoods. As such, white police officers use force 60 percent more than Black police officers, and use gun force twice as often. CRT explains why. Developing a *Criminal Justice Action Kit* largely directed at Black males, the New York City Department of Public Health (2019) stipulated to the negative impact between policing and public health, reporting that populations targeted by the police have a higher risk for chronic mental and physical health conditions. CRT explains why.

According to the U.S. Department of Justice (2018, p. 1) report, *Contacts Between Police and the Public*, police used physical force against nearly 1 million people in the United States and Black people (5.2%), specifically Black men, were more likely to experience police violence than anyone else in the nation. Again, CRT explains why. Justin Feldman (2015), in *Public Health and the Policing of Black Lives*, added:

> While current public health literature on policing is sparse, it points to numerous adverse health impacts. Research has shown that police crackdowns dissuade

injection drug users from carrying clean needles, stop-and-frisk programs induce post-traumatic stress in their black and Latino targets, police presence in hospitals deters black men on probation or parole from using emergency rooms, police enforcement against sex workers creates riskier occupational conditions, and police officers kill black people at a disproportionately higher rates as compared to whites. Additional research on the health effects of policing would greatly benefit discussions about both law enforcement and public health, but these studies are difficult to conduct because there is a widespread unwillingness on the part of police departments to share data with the public. (para. 3)

CRT argues that policing is colorism. CRT argues that policing is gentrification. CRT argues that policing is a public health issue. CRT argues that policing is colonization. CRT argues that policing is food and water deserts. CRT argues that policing is mass incarceration. CRT argues that policing is a permanent manifestation of white Americans' anger, rage, fear, and erotic desire for Black bodies. CRT argues that policing is white America. CRT argues for self-determination. CRT argues for revolution. CRT argues that policing must be dismantled and abolished.

CRT must be seen, heard, and absorbed through a new, revolutionary, and liberatory set of Pan-Afrikan eyes, ears, and souls—*rituals*—inspired by what Ture (1967, 1971) described as organizing an Afrikan resistance consciousness. Ture (1971) argued that there were five primary lessons that Black people must learn from the revolutionary Black Power Movement of the 1960s, with one of them being the role the academy must play in Black liberation. Ture (1971) argued that the vast body of knowledge shared through the halls of academia has one single purpose: to alleviate the suffering of humanity. In my work (Gaskew, 2014a,b, 2018, 2020a,b), I described how Black liberation is synergized with Black power and that knowledge is Black power. In fact, all knowledge is inevitably transformed into Black political power; thus, when Jamil Abdullah al-Amin (1969, p. 1) echoed, "Every Black birth in America is political. With each new birth comes a potential challenge to the existing order. Each new generation brings forth untested militancy," he understood the synergistic connection between knowledge and Black power. As the mothers and fathers of humanity, Ture (1967, 1971) argued that all Afrikan people, Black people, Pan-Afrikan people are the vanguards and benefactors of this knowledge. Thus, the knowledge acquired in the academy, by way of scholarship that reflects the Black radical tradition, belongs to the Black masses in America, and thus is designed to be used for the benefit of the Black masses of the world. As a student of Ture (1967, 1971), I argue throughout this book that CRT, shaped and formed by Black thought, serves as the intellectual language of Black liberation. Thus, CRT will be used to alleviate the suffering of Black humanity, through the application of police abolition.

However, one of the most significant impediments to applying CRT to policing comes by way of the academy's very own systemic violence, which intentionally limits "Black voices" within the academic discipline of criminal justice. Today, less than 5 percent of all tenure-stream faculty positions in criminal justice/criminology across the countries 826 bachelor's programs, 299 master's programs, and 39 doctoral programs in criminal justice/criminology are Black scholars (Greene, Gabbidon, & Wilson, 2018). In fact, Black males make up less than 2 percent of full professors within the academic discipline of criminal justice. For over a century, universities routinely denied access to criminal justice erudition to Black intellectuals. As a result, over 85 percent of all criminal justice professors nationwide today are white. Just imagine the inherent damage white supremacy has done to Black contributions to criminological thought, research, and scholarship related to Black liberation. Policing may have been abolished decades ago if Black scholars had access to these academic spaces. As a Black male, a full professor of criminal justice, and a director of a criminal justice program, occupying intellectual spaces where only a handful of Black scholars sit, I have a duty to advance the Black radical tradition and apply scholarship that leads to Black liberation (Gaskew, 2020a,b).

We must know and accept that CRT is the language of Black liberation. Applying CRT is the first component in the process of police abolition. CRT speaks the language of police abolition. CRT tells us why policing must be abolished. CRT compels us to "confront critically the most explosive issue in American civilization"—the historical greed, actionable ignorance, and willful hate of the institution of policing in becoming the face of white supremacy (Crenshaw, Gotanda, Peller, & Thomas, 1995, p. xi; Gaskew, 2018, 2020a,b). CRT permits us to examine the role of policing in the "construction and maintenance of white social domination and subordination" of Black lives (Crenshaw, Gotanda, Peller, & Thomas, 1995, p. xi; Gaskew, 2018, 2020a,b). CRT provides an empirical framework for the Black masses to clearly understand that policing in America can never be reformed. That policing in America can never be made more efficient, more effective, or more ecological for the existence of Black lives (Gaskew, 2018, 2020a,b). That policing in America can never be more than a permanent fixture of racism, with the goal of economic exploitation and extermination of Black bodies, under the evil of the mental, physical, and spiritual lie of white domination (Gaskew, 2014a, 2018, 2020a,b). That policing in America can only be dismantled (Gaskew, 2018, 2020a,b). That policing in America must be abolished. You see, CRT provides the baseline for Black liberation.

CRT explains why the white liberal reform platforms of hiring more Black police chiefs, Black prosecutors, Black judges, and Black prison wardens will never rid the criminal justice system in America of racism. CRT explains that American policing is white supremacy and that using a Black face as a spokesperson does not negate this premise. Franz Fanon (1952) openly shared this truth in *Black Skin, White Masks*. CRT provides an empirical foundation that abolition is the only solution to policing, under a platform of examining several core themes: (1) To understand how a regime of white supremacy and its subordination of Black people has been created and maintained in American policing. (2) The desire not merely to understand the vexed bond between policing and racial power but to abolish the institution of policing. (3) CRT is about storytelling and every single Black body in America has a collective story on policing. (4) It critiques liberalism and how it has provided affirmative action, color blind, anti-bias training cover for policing. (5) CRT seeks answers by exposing the psychology of race, white self-interest, the politics of colonialism and anti-colonialism, or other sources of police-generated white supremacy. (6) It seeks to understand the underpinnings of how policing is structurally married to racism. (7) CRT explains the intersection between race, sex, class, and police oppression. (8) CRT analyzes the synergy of police essentialism and Black colonialism. (9) It dissects the Black radical tradition of cultural nationalism/separatism as it relates to police oppression. (10) CRT explains Black representation within a policing state, that is, what role should Black people in America play in policing and abolishing policing (Crenshaw, Gotanda, Peller, & Thomas, 1995, p. xiii; Gaskew, 2018, pp. 187–199, 2020a,b). CRT intellectually peels back the multilayered null hypothesis of police reformation. CRT provides the metaphysical language for unfriending policing.

Chapter 2

Unfriending Policing

Being called a nigger by a Chicago Police Officer was not unusual back in 1973, even as a child. Although most of the time it was normally mumbled or mentioned as a side-note, this white police officer wanted to let a nine-year old Black male, in his eyes a man-child, know that "nigger" was going to be used as a weapon of intimidation and violence on the CPD use of force continuum, just like a canine, pepper spray, Taser, or an AR-15 semiautomatic assault style rifle. When it happened, I wasn't surprised. I was already culturally resistant to white police officers and their twenty-four-hour a day, seven days a week bullshit hustle. In my mind, he was just another chump, in a very long line of chumps with badges and guns talking shit. It didn't scare me. I had unfriended policing by birthright.

DECOLONIZATION: CONVERTING
THE UNCONSCIOUS TO THE CONSCIOUS

Kwame Ture (2003) noted that when a Black child is born, a Yoruba West African ritual requires that a birth poem or birth praise song be composed in the newborn's honor. This birth ritual is called *oriki*. Ture (2003) stated:

> Some days later at the naming ceremony by which the infant is ushered formally into its place in human society, the child's oriki is recited publicly, first into the ear of the child and then to the assembled community of family and neighbors. The first language a child will be required to commit to memory, the oriki imprints the child with its complex historical, spiritual, and social identities. . . . It is at once prayer, thanksgiving, celebration, and prophecy. It is a meditation on the meaning and significance of the new human's name. It is an evocation

of the strong deeds, character, and praise names of the infant's ancestors, and, perhaps most important, it is an optimistic attempt to project in desirable ways the child's future personality and life prospects. By evoking linage, the oriki is ultimately about spiritual inheritance: that eternal life force that has many names, which we receive from our ancestors. A vital force of which we, in each generation, are only the contemporary incarnations. And which in turn we pass on to our children and they to theirs, so that the lineage never dies. Oriki, while memory and history, is also character, at once both individual and collective. We as Africans know that each individual one of us is ultimately the sum of that long line of ancestors—spiritual forces and moral arbiters—who have gone before to produce us. The psychic forces out of which we all come. Oriki is a salute to family. It is also an inheritance one requires at birth. No one composes his or her own. I have myself written this section, it is in its own way a kind of oriki, a salute to roots, origins, and family. (pp. 11–12)

The second ritual in the process of dismantling the institution of policing in America is part of the Black diaspora's collective cosmic spiritual inheritance of liberation: to unfriend policing. That is, to come to a conscious awareness that the institution of policing in American will never play a role in the universal growth of the Black body, mind, or spirit; thus, we need to decolonize ourselves from policing and its influences in or around our psychic lives. Ture (1967) described this process as moving from *unconsciousness to consciousness*. James Baldwin (1961) believed that Black people are the consciousness of America and that to be Black and conscious in America is to be in a constant state of healing and resistance (Somé, 1998; Gaskew, 2018, 2020a). Revolutionary Black consciousness is at the forefront of mitigating the uncontrolled desires of greed, anger, and ignorance (Williams, 2000). Revolutionary Black consciousness is the physical, psychological, and spiritual heartbeat of truth and justice. Revolutionary Black consciousness is the voice for the voiceless. Revolutionary Black consciousness serves as the vanguard dark matter for liberation movements around the world searching for answers to human pain and suffering. Abolishing policing is a natural extension of Black liberation. Revolutionary Black consciousness purges the Black diaspora of the fear of abolishing policing. The Black Liberation Army (1971) argues:

Our [Black diaspora] social/psychotic fear of the racists ruling circles must be purged . . . and only by developing our capacity to fight our enemy will this unreasonable and reactionary fear be eradicated from our social psyche. Revolutionary violence is not so much a self-cleansing process as it is a necessary ingredient in creating a psychological frame of mind amongst the ruling classes that our liberation must be granted. (p. 14)

As an Afrikan man born in America in the early 1960s, I saw firsthand the incredible life force of Black consciousness with the *Ari* of the Black Power Movement, giving birth to a generation of *urban shaman* (King, 1990) who immersed themselves in the collective goals echoed by Karenga (2010): to solve pressing problems within the Black community and to continue the revolutionary struggle being waged to end white supremacy, racism, and oppression against Black spaces. A Black consciousness liberates us from the colonizing impact of policing (Gaskew, 2018, pp. 189–190, 2020a).

Unfriending policing requires a metaphysical understanding that we do not need the police for anything. Absolutely nothing. That American policing can play no role in Black lives. The Black diaspora must stop making excuses for calling the police. Don't call the police for anything, anyplace, or anytime, ever. We must acknowledge that policing is a white supremacist constructed humiliation designed to despiritualize the richness, beauty, and essence of Blackness, and we, the Pan-Afrikan masses, must physically, mentally, and spiritually reject everything about policing (Gaskew, 2018, 2020a,b). This rejection of policing must be whole and part of what Williams (2000, 2016) describes as an *enlightened awakening*: conscious rituals designed for the recovery of *our* memory and the reaffirmation of *our* life purpose as the Earth's first human beings (pp. 32–36). Rituals that recover the memory of our consciousness. Rituals that reaffirm our consciousness. Rituals that heal the colonizing effects of policing from our consciousness. Rituals that detox the addictive poisons of policing's psychic domination from our consciousness.

OUR MELANIN

According to Llaila Afrika (2009, pp. 4–27), in *Melanin: What Makes Black People Black*, melanin is the biochemical substance that drives physical, mental, emotional, and spiritual life for Black people in America. Melanin is the universe's natural biochemical resistance to American policing. It is the biochemical version of the Black radical tradition. Thus, the key to controlling Afrikan people in America is to reduce their connection to their biochemical Blackness. Afrika (2009, pp. 4–27) believes that our undereducation, dis-education, dysfunction, and miseducation about melanin reflect white domi-nation, post-traumatic colonialism trauma, and post-traumatic slavery trauma. Afrika (2009) argues that it is no accident that the aboriginal people on the planet, Black people, have the highest amount of the biochemical pigment of melanin. That melanin is a civilizing chemical and reproduces itself. That melanin is the vital chemical that makes life itself. Afrika (2009) suggests that melanin absorbs all types of energy such as sunlight, electromagnetic, music heard by the human ear and sounds the human ear cannot hear, phone waves, radio waves, radar, computer radiation, X-ray, cosmic rays, ultraviolet rays, heat waves, microwaves, and so forth. That melanin uses the energy in the total environment, such as water energy, earth, moon, sun, galaxy, cycles of planets, cycles of minerals, and so forth. Afrika (2009, pp. 4–27) notes that the color of melanin appears as Black because it absorbs all colors. It is a cellular Black hole similar to Black holes in outer space. The sun and sunlight sit at the center of this power. As we know, the sun radiates the full color spectrum of light. Afrika (2009) argues that the full spectrum light striking the eye's retina nerve stimulates the production of melanin and that a polluted environment, whether land, water, noise pollution, negative energy, lack of exercise, processed foods, synthetic drugs, or even communities that contain American policing, negatively impacts the life force of melanin. Afrika (2009, pp. 4–27) debates that this is the reason why Afrikans in America are placed in carceral facilities, especially solitary confinement, unnatural conditions that deprive natural sunlight, in order to kill their melanin.

Kamene (2019, p. 29) suggests that melanin unifies all living organisms. Afrika (2009) argues that melanin is the biochemical substance that synchronizes the rhythmicity of the Black body. In doing so, melanin regulates the Afrikan cycle of consciousness: unconscious to conscious thought. This rhythmicity sits at the heart of the Black radical tradition. Melanin feeds the heightened ability to create spontaneously, to improvise, in all Afrikan people. Thus, melanin is the primary controller of human creativity and human culture: music, dance, acting, dress styles, hair styles, language usage, inventions, science, arts, and culture. By extension naturally, melanin is the primary controller of the universal virtues of truth, justice, balance, harmony, order, righteousness, and reciprocity. Afrika (2009) cautions that the universal poisons, greed, anger, and ignorance, are anti-melanin and therefore anti-Black culture. Thus, the *Ari* or Karma behind the deeds that cater to these poisons, specifically when they are directed at Black people by Black people, have powerful negative spiritual energies and metaphysical consequences. Melanin sits at the heart of life's chemistry, or what we know as *Keme*, from both a physical and a metaphysical state. Afrika (2009) states that Afrikans are born with the ability to reach metaphysical states of time and place. Melanin creates Black consciousness. Black consciousness is a cultural element. Culture educates a person to have awareness and awareness gives consciousness. Culture gives a person a belief system and beliefs give a person emotion. Afrikan people in America are tied to their own culture. They are drawn to it like a magnet. It's embedded into the Black unconscious.

Finally, Afrika (2009) argues that melanin has a *free radical behavior.* Melanin naturally resists harmful synthetic chemicals to Black bodies, and within this metaphysical space, melanin naturally resists synthetic systems to

Black bodies, such as policing. Melanin is the body's biochemical *spiritual inheritance*. It connects the mental, physical, and spiritual DNA of the Black diaspora. This metaphysical spiritual inheritance forms the psychic core of unfriending policing in America (Afrika, 2009, pp. 4–27).

OUR *MA'AT*

According to Hilliard, Williams, & Damali (1987, pp. 1–15) in *The Teachings of Ptahhotep: The Oldest Book in the World*, Black people created the concept of justice on this planet. Black people created the Kemetic and pre-Kemetic understanding of our universe, where the first civilizations were native Afrikan. The world knows this location as Kemet or Egypt. That means that the world's first civilization was a Black civilization. The world knows this as truth. The colonization of Africa, the enslavement of Afrikan people, and the segregation of Afrikans in the Afrikan Diaspora were accompanied by a wholesale, systematic falsification of human record. Ancient Kemet provided a set of values and a code of behaviors by which to live one's life in the world before death. No higher human behavioral code has been found anywhere in human history than the earliest code of the ancient Kemites. Thus, we are guided in essence by forty-two declarations of virtues. A set of values and principles that serve as the foundation of the world's moral standard for the art of life. This concept of justice is reflected in the principles of *ma'at* (pp.14–15).

Muata Ashby (2005, pp. 18–138) in *Introduction to MA'AT Philosophy* describes *Ma'at* as a spiritual inheritance based on seven core universal virtues: *truth, justice, balance, harmony, order, righteousness*, and *reciprocity*. Anubis Hotep (2016, pp. 155–164) in *The Book of Ma'at* speaks of seven interconnected principles: *psychokinesis, correspondence, vibration, opposition, rhythm, cause and effect, and gender*. Those who live by *ma'at* discover and know truth. *Ma'at* is the cosmic principle of order and harmony and a philosophy for attaining that order and harmony, which leads to balance and divine peace. Ashby (2005) argues that *ma'at* represents the very order which constitutes creation. Creation itself is *ma'at*. It refers to a deep understanding of divinity and the manner in which virtuous qualities can be developed in the human heart so as to come closer to the Divine. Thus, *ma'at* is a philosophy, a spiritual symbol, as well as a cosmic energy force which provides life to the entire universe. *Ma'at* is the aboriginal *lady justice*. She is the symbolic embodiment of world order, justice, correctness, and peace. She is known by her headdress composed of a feather of truth. She is a form of the Goddess Aset, who represents wisdom and spiritual awakening through balance and equanimity (Ashby, 2005; Hotep, 2016).

Kamene (2019) describes this Kemetic energy in terms of science and spirituality. The life cycle of the Black diaspora is an unbreakable combination of the two, with science being matter, finity and light, while spirituality, revealing space, infinity, and darkness (pp. 2–3). That science and spirituality create the platform for knowledge, ritual, wisdom, and justice. Kamene (2019) argued that our purpose in life was guided through the prism of science and spirituality, by way of evolution and involution with evolution being "the life history, growth, and perfection of the physical human body from its very beginning" and involution, "the history of the internal search for the Creator within" (p. 9). The Black diaspora, as the first human beings, understood the connection between the earthly physical and the organic cosmic. That our cosmic responsibility is to uncover our unique purpose; however, this gift will lay dormant until activated by consciousness (p. 43).

Ashby (2005) suggests that in ancient Kemet, the judges and all those connected with the justice system were initiated into the teachings of *ma'at*. Thus, those who would discharge the laws and regulations of society were well trained in the Afrikan ethical and spiritual-mystical values of life, fairness, justice, and the responsibility to serve society in order to promote harmony in society, and the possibility for spiritual development in an atmosphere of freedom and peace. For only when there is justice and fairness in society, can there be an abiding harmony and peace. Policing in America and its actors will never be able to live up to these moral and ethical standards. Ashby (2005) also reminds us that *ma'at* encompasses the teachings of *Ari* and reincarnation, or the destiny of every individual based on past actions, thoughts, and feelings. Ari also refers to the belief that one's actions lead to certain experiences and consequences. In mystical terms, the heart is the metaphor of the human mind including the conscious, subconscious, and unconscious levels. The mind is the reservoir of all your ideas, convictions, and feelings. The heart is the sum total of your experiences, actions, aspirations, and your conscience of Ari, and these are judged in the balance against the feather of *ma'at*. Thus, *Ari* or Karma should be thought of as the total effect of a person's actions and conduct during the successive phases of their existence (p. 81). Since *ma'at* is the personification of justice and righteousness upon which the *Life Force* or *Supreme Being* has created the universe, it is *ma'at* who judges the soul. *Ma'at* judges the heart (unconscious mind) of the collective in an attempt to determine to what extent the heart has lived in accordance with truth, correctness, reality, genuineness, uprightness, righteousness, justice, steadfastness, and the unalterable nature of creation. Policing holds none of these sacred principles of sustaining equitable human life. Policing will never understand the Black diaspora gift and cosmological space of *ma'at*. Therefore, American policing must be abolished. Ashby (2009) makes this perfectly clear as he dissects the metaphysical nature of *ma'at*.

Theophile Obenga (2015, pp. 103–119), in *African Philosophy*, argues that *ma'at*, a concept known throughout the Black Afrikn culture as *truth*, is designed in pursuit of knowledge and happiness. That *ma'at* serves as the leading principle of all of society, connecting Kemet with the entire universe. Obenga (2015) argues that *ma'at* is Afrikan philosophy or the Afrikan world-view. "*Ma'at* is the blood vessels which bring vital life fluids to the cultural body of Afrikan people as they enter each new era of struggle. . . . It is the only medicine that works to restore the modern Afrikan mind" (p. 111). Ashby (2005) believes that when one comes into harmony with *ma'at*, one is coming into harmony with the balance of the cosmos. That is, the human being is not simply a mind and a body which will someday cease to exist. Every human being's mind and body are emanations or expressions of their eternal soul. The mind and body are referred to as the *ego-personality*, and it is this ego-personality that is temporal and mortal. The soul is immortal. The ego-personality is the subject of error, confusion, and the consequences of these imperfections. Ashby (2009) states that if a human being is aware of the deeper soul-reality, this state of being is known as the state of enlightenment. However, if one does not have knowledge and experience of their higher self, then they exist in a condition of ignorance, which will lead to sinful behavior, pain, and sorrow. Understanding that the ego-personality is subject to the forces of time and space and will suffer the consequences of its actions becomes the foundational basis for the teachings of *Ari* or Karma. This cosmological reality becomes a critical factor in the Black diaspora unfriending policing. Afrikans in America must understand that *Ari* is a cosmological weapon for liberation and must be used against policing and its systemic actors. Black people must allow policing and its systemic actors, which are only human beings that form their own synthetic ego-personality, to face their collective Ari. Ashby (2005) adds when the ego-personality dies, the soul moves on. If the human being has discovered their higher self, purified the heart, for example, mind and body, then the soul moves forward to unite with the supreme self or God. If the ego in an actor is fettered in ignorance, then the soul moves in an astral plane until it finds another ego-personality about to be born again in the world of time and space so that it may have an opportunity to have experiences that will lead it to discover its higher nature. This is the basis for the teaching of reincarnation (Ashby, 2005, pp. 18–138; Hotep, 2016, pp. 155–164). The actors of policing are trapped in a cycle of violent ignorance, anger, fear, and greed, where every rebirth simply adds to their legacy of pain and suffering. Unfriending policing would be cosmological justice.

Ashby (2005) argues that positive impressions are developed through positive actions, such as by living a life of righteousness. That negative impressions are developed through negative actions, such as by living a life of anger, fear, ignorance, and greed. Policing is the personification of anger, fear, ignorance, and greed. American policing is the personification of unrighteousness. *Ma'at* is the orderly flow of energy which maintains the universe. This universe does not include American policing. This natural process represents the flow of creation wherein there is a constant movement and a balancing of opposites: the cosmological yin and yang. Policing will never be part of this cosmological balance. In ordinary human life, those who have not achieved the state of enlightenment perceive nature as a conglomeration of forces which are unpredictable and in need of control. Policing and its actors will never achieve a state of enlightenment. As Earth's aboriginal people, we know that as our spiritual sensitivity matures, as a collective, we realize that what once appeared to be chaotic is in reality the divine plan of the Supreme Being in the process of unfoldment. When this state of consciousness is attained, we realize that there is an underlying order in nature which can only be perceived with spiritual eyes. Thus, as Black people in America, when we attune our own sense of order and balance with the cosmic order, a spontaneous unity occurs between us and the cosmos, and the principles of *ma'at* become a part of one's inner character and proceed from one in a spontaneous manner. This means that through the deeper understanding of cosmic order and by the practice of living in harmony with that order, the Black diaspora will have mental and spiritual peace and harmony. Ashby (2005, pp. 18–138) believes that it is this peace and harmony which allows the mind to become a mirror in which the soul is able to realize its oneness with the universal soul. American policing can never produce peace and harmony. Policing can only serve as a physical, mental, and spiritual impediment to peace and harmony.

Ma'at is the Black diaspora cosmological weapon against policing. Does this make sense yet? Ashby (2005) argues that the universe bases its decisions about one's fate, by examining one's collective record as a human being. Understanding this truth, how could any Black person in America not demand for the abolition of policing? Since mystical philosophy maintains that happiness can only come from self-knowledge, whether cosmic or Devine consciousness, and not from worldly pursuits, all egoistic actions will inevitably lead to disappointment, if not in this lifetime, in a future one. Ashby (2005) reminds us that if this sounds like Buddhism, Taoism, or Indian Dharma, all of their roots can be found within the Black diaspora. You see, true happiness is defined as an experience of the state of enlightenment, whereby one experiences joy all the time, in all conditions and circumstances. True happiness is a state of being. When an enlightened person performs actions, they are not doing so to become happy as a result, but because it is righteous action that they are being guided to be so by their connection to the divine; thus, in effect, they are performing divinely ordained works. Black people, by their aboriginal righteous nature and by their aboriginal righteous actions, reject American policing. Within the context of white supremacy, policing is a state of being. True happiness within the Black diaspora and American policing cannot live within the same state of being. Ari impels a person to reincarnate in order to attempt the fulfillment of the desire left over from the previous Karma, and this cycle of birth, death, birth continues until there is full self-knowledge of the illusoriness of desires, worldly attainments, and actions. Thus, Ashby (2005) explains that Ari is not fate but the tendency that a person sets up, in their deep unconscious to like or dislike and desire or repudiate. The Black radical tradition is part of our Ari. Our Ari is the abolishment of policing. The implication is that we reap (harvest) the result of our state of mind (heart). Our state of mind, including our subconscious feelings and desires, is weighed against cosmic order. Therefore, one controls one's own fate according to one's level of wisdom or reasoning capacity. The fate and cosmic order of the Black diaspora demands the abolition of policing.

Ashby (2005) reminds us that when the practice of *ma'at* is perfected, the mind becomes calm. This calmness allows the soul to cease its identification with the thoughts and the mind, and to behold its true nature as an entity separate from our greed and ego-self. The soul is now free to expand its vision beyond the constructive pettiness of human desires and mental agitation, in order to behold the expansion of the inner self. It is in this place of calmness that we find the collective clarity to unfriend policing. This calmness reflects our love for the universe and all living beings. Policing by its synthetic origins jeopardizes any realm of calmness. According to Ashby (2005) everything is action. Black resistance is action. Black revolution is action. Black knowledge is action. Black power is action. Unfriending policing is action. It follows that if you undertake Black spaces for absorbing knowledge and practicing that knowledge, those same actions will lead you to liberation from state bondage. Policing is state bondage. Ignorance of your true self, the aboriginal spiritual inheritance of Afrika, is the root cause of the bondage to the Karmic cycle of structural violence. Thus, a radical resistance, a metaphysical revolution against policing, is a requirement for Black liberation. Radical resistance to policing removes the karmic cycle of structural violence. Revolution is a call to wake up from this delusion of pain and suffering. Revolution is in reality prosperity, because it stimulates the mind through suffering so that it may look for a higher vision of life and discover the abode of true happiness, peace, and contentment which transcends worldly measure. The accumulation of pain and suffering that the Black diaspora has endured at the hands of American policing has provided the Black collective with the spiritual enlightenment of breaking the psychological chains of policing.

Can any white person in America even attempt to imagine themselves in the position of Black people within the cruel and criminalized narrative that policing has created for our bodies, minds, spirits, and give us a common sense, logical, and rational methodology of how we should deal with a system of oppression that, by design, creates psychic violence? We must unfriend policing. Black people must remember that liberation has always lived in the deepest part of our consciousness souls. The aboriginal Black diaspora has been created to uphold the order of the universe. American policing will never serve such a role. As the vanguards of the planet, the Black diaspora is tasked with assisting in the support and positive evolution of the universe. This is the underlying core of justice. This is why my ancestors required me to sacrifice my life's work for justice, fighting on the front lines against white supremacy. *Ma'at* requires that you always strive to perform work that is in harmony with your nature. Many people suffer through life because they have made wrong choices about their profession or occupation and because they feel stuck and are unable to change their lot in life. The Black diaspora must accept that their task is to go beyond the fears of human existence. Black people are children of the universe, and when you tread the path of truth, even though it may be difficult at times, it is our cosmological destiny. This is our spiritual inheritance. This is our Black radical tradition. The actions of a living being in *Ma'at* should always include *selfless service*:

- Give righteousness, order and truth to humanity.
- Give food to the hungry. Give water to the thirsty.
- Give shelter to the homeless.
- Give comfort to the weepers.
- Give protection to the weak from the strong.
- Give wisdom to the ignorant; and
- Give opportunity to the discouraged. (Ashby, 2005, pp. 123–124)

Selfless service will never be a virtue of American policing. Selfless service is a cornerstone of Blackness. Selfless service is one of the greatest and the most secure methods of purifying the heart (becoming virtuous), because it makes one humble and it effaces the ego. Instead, policing is trapped in the cycle of violence:

- Anger
- Hate
- Frustration
- Negative actions
- Greed
- Passion
- Weak will
- Irrationality
- Ignorance. (Ashby, 2005. p. 135)

The root cause of violence is not understanding your purpose, that is, ignorance of one's true identity as being one with the life force. American policing has no universal purpose within *ma'at*. American policing and those actors that support its narrative live in a state of ignorance. American policing is not selfless service. Within *ma'at*, American policing is a universal crime. The central theme is that all life, all existence is indeed part of one whole, one essence, one being. There is always a witness to the universal crime of policing. The Black diaspora serves as these witnesses. Black people will always draw upon the metaphysical power of *Mantu* and *Ogun*. The universe is the eternal watcher who makes sure that a person never escapes from the repercussions of their actions. This is the divine law of Ari. This is the divine law of Karma. If all creation is one whole and the Black diaspora is the aboriginal human part of that whole, then how can American policing and its actors ever be part of this collective whole? As a community, it is our cosmological duty to eradicate the seeds of violence. It is our cosmological duty to unfriend and dismantle the institution of American policing.

WHAT WE WANT NOW: WHAT WE BELIEVE

According to Joshua Bloom and Waldo Martin (2016), in *Black Against Empire: The History and Politics of the Black Panther Party*, and Joshua Anderson (2012, pp. 249–267), in *A Tension in the Political Thought of Huey P. Newton. Journal of African American Studies*, the Ten-Point Program is a set of moral guidelines designed to remind the Black diaspora to live by and actively practice the Black radical tradition of resistance. Reading it today, it clearly serves as a karmic blueprint for unfriending the police. Each word, sentence, and paragraph are designed to metaphysically remind Black people of the importance of securing a life without the construct of state oppression. The document was created by the founders of the BPP, Huey P. Newton and Bobby Seale, whose political and cultural thoughts lay within the revolutionary realm of Black anarchism and Black nationalism. The Ten-Point Program was released on May 15, 1967, in the second issue of the party's weekly newspaper *The Black Panther*. All succeeding 537 issues contained the platform "What We Want Now!" The program comprised two sections: The first section "What We Want Now!" described the political and cultural demands of the BPP from the systemic base of American white supremacy. The second section "What We Believe" additionally outlined the philosophical views of the party and the much broader Black Power Movement of the 1960s. The platform provided a rough draft of the abolitionist language that we know today as *critical race theory*. It set the metaphysical tone of truth, justice, balance, harmony, order, righteousness, and reciprocity, the cornerstones of *ma'at*, within the Black Power Movement. It framed the narrative of Black decolonization as a critical element of Black liberation. It demanded that the Black diaspora control the application of justice within its own communities. It argued the benefits of the physical, psychic, and spiritual power of armed resistance against police violence.

According to *The Black Panther* (1967), the party's biweekly community newsletter, the platform consisted of the following:

What We Want Now!

1. We want freedom. We want power to determine the destiny of our Black community.
2. We want full employment for our people.
3. We want an end to the robbery by the white men of our Black community.
4. We want decent housing, fit for shelter of human beings.
5. We want education for our people that exposes the true nature of this decadent American society. We want education that teaches us our true history and our role in the present-day society.
6. We want all Black men to be exempt from military service.
7. We want an immediate end to police brutality and murder of Black people.
8. We want freedom for all Black men held in federal, state, county, and city prisons and jails.
9. We want all Black people when brought to trial to be tried in court by a jury of their peer group or people from their Black communities, as defined by the constitution of the United States.
10. We want land, bread, housing, education, clothing, justice and peace. (p. 3)

What We Believe!

1. We believe that Black people will not be free until we are able to determine our own destiny.
2. We believe that the federal government is responsible and obligated to give every man employment or a guaranteed income. We believe that if the white American business men will not give full employment, the means of production should be taken from the businessmen and placed in the community so that the people of the community can organize and employ all of its people and give a high standard of living.
3. We believe that this racist government has robbed us and now we are demanding the overdue debt of forty acres and two mules. We will accept the payment in currency which will be distributed to our many communities. The American racist has taken part in the slaughter of over

50,000,000 Black people; therefore, we feel that this is a modest demand that we make.

4. We believe that if the white landlords will not give decent housing to our Black community, then the housing and the land should be made into cooperatives so that our community, with government aid, can build and make a decent housing for its people.

5. We believe in an educational system that will give our people a knowledge of self. If a man does not have knowledge of himself and his position in society and the world, then he has little chance to relate to anything else.

6. We believe that Black people should not be forced to fight in the military service to defend a racist government that does not protect us. We will not fight and kill other people of color in the world who, like Black people, are being victimized by the white racist government of America. We will protect ourselves from the force and violence of the racist police and the racist military, by whatever means necessary.

7. We believe we can end police brutality in our Black community by organizing Black self-defense groups that are dedicated to defending our Black community from racist police oppression and brutality. The second Amendment of the Constitution of the United States gives us the right to bear arms. We therefore believe that all Black people should arm themselves for self-defense.

8. We believe that all Black people should be released from the many jails and prisons because they have not received a fair and impartial trial.

9. We believe that the courts should follow the United States Constitution so that Black people will receive fair trials. The 14th Amendment of the US Constitution gives a man a right to be tried by his peers. A peer is a person from a similar economic, social, religious, geographical, environmental, historical, and racial background. To do this the court will be forced to select a jury from the Black community from which the Black defendant came. We have been, and are being, tried by all-white juries that have no understanding of "the average reasoning man" of the Black community.

10. When in the course of human events, it becomes necessary for one people to dissolve the political bonds which have connected them with another, and to assume among the powers of the earth, the separate and equal station to which the laws of nature and nature's god entitle them, a decent respect to the opinions of mankind requires that they should declare the causes which impel them to separation. We hold these truths to be self-evident, and that all men are created equal, that they are endowed by their creator with certain unalienable rights, that

among these are life, liberty, and the pursuit of happiness. That to secure these rights, governments are instituted among men, deriving their just powers from the consent of the governed, that whenever any form of government becomes destructive of these ends, it is the right of the people to alter or abolish it, and to institute new government, laying its foundation on such principles and organizing its power in such a form as to them shall seem most likely to effect their safety and happiness. Prudence, indeed, will dictate that governments long established should not be changed for light and transient causes; and accordingly, all experience hath shewn, that mankind are more disposed to suffer, while evils are sufferable, than to right themselves by abolishing the forms to which they are accused. But when a long train of abuses and usurpations, pursuing invariably the same object, evinces a design to reduce them under absolute despotism, it is their right, and their duty, to throw off such government, and to provide new guards of their future security. (p. 3)

Although the various concepts outlined in "What We Want Now!" and "What We Believe!" resonate throughout this book, I cannot overemphasize the specific influence of their underlying themes that address (1) an educational iris for critical race studies; (2) a metaphysical nature in dismantling systems of oppression; (3) a rejection on white narratives of politics and culture; (4) requiring community-controlled forms of justice; and (5) a natural right of armed resistance. The BPP created a revolutionary platform that can be translated as a blueprint for police abolition. I will examine this further in the upcoming chapters.

According to Owusu Yaki Yakubu (1981), in *On Transforming the Colonial and Criminal Mentality*, unfriending policing is a revolutionary and decolonizing action. As such, El-Hajj Malik El-Shabazz (1964) believed that:

Revolutions are fought to get control of land, to remove the absentee landlord and gain control of the land and the institutions that flow from that land. . . . You also have a people today who not only know what they want, but also know what they are supposed to have. And they themselves are creating another generation that . . . will be ready and willing to do whatever is necessary to see that what they should have materializes immediately. (para. 50)

Those *lands* are Black neighborhoods, those *landlords* are the police, and those *institutions* are the American white supremacist systems that legitimize them. Those *generations* are the Black masses today. What is *necessary* is police abolition.

Again, a clear distinction must be made when defining revolution and rebellion with regard to abolishing policing. Rebellion does not signify abolition. A rebellion is generally just an attack on individual police actions, such as the shooting death of a Black person at the hands of the police, which is usually spontaneous, short-lived, and without the purpose of combatting state systems of rule. Rebellion simply brings into question the methods of white supremacy but stop well short of dismantling its white power structure, which is the foundation of its legitimacy. Rebellion exposes intolerable conditions and treatment, such as stop and frisk, but does not declare war on the system that is responsible for supporting these slave patrol tactics. A rebellion essentially wants to reform elements of policing, still leaving the entire policing industrial complex intact.

A revolution, on the other hand, seeks not merely to reform policing but to completely systemically unfriend and abolish it. I fully acknowledge the seduction of rebellion over revolution in American policing because of the widespread colonized belief that reform can be made as simply as mobilizing a protest against police brutality or by electing a Black progressive district attorney. You see, reform allows Black liberals to play revolutionary and to engage in acts of adventurism or confrontation, which looks great when raising one's profile on Black twitter or securing funding from a white liberal nonprofit organization. These *demonstrations of impulse* against policing are always much easier to mobilize and undertake, rather than a protracted unfriending process toward abolishing policing, because there is little or no actual risk. Everyone knows what I'm talking about. On a daily basis, Black liberal activists mobilize demonstrations against the police in some form or fashion; however, they demand that all participants remain peaceful and nonviolent while working collectively with the police to ensure state-controlled pacifist compliance. They would never dare mobilize any mass event without the full consent and active participation of their very own slave patrols, because of the fear of appearing to have any sense of Black power. Black power is revolution and revolution is Black power. The overwhelming majority of Black liberal activists are *more police than the police*. Unfriending policing requires an unmitigating display of metaphysical Black power.

SHIFTING FROM THE PHYSICAL
TO THE METAPHYSICAL

According to Malidoma Patrice Somé (1998), in *The Healing Wisdom of Africa: Finding Life Purpose through Nature, Ritual, and Community*, and Angel Williams, in *Being Black: Zen and the Art of Living with Fearlessness and Grace* (2000) and *Radical Dharma: Talking Race, Love, and Liberation* (2016), the art of healing, that is the universe's gift to living beings that allow us to move forward physically and metaphysically through our pain and suffering, begins and ends with the noble virtue of truth. The pain and suffering caused by policing Black bodies over the last four centuries are both physical and metaphysical in nature, scope, and understanding; thus, it's only logical that a Black ontological lens be used in seeking liberation from American policing.

According to Mumia Abu-Jamal (2003), in *Faith of Our Fathers: An Examination of the Spiritual Life of Africa*, without a doubt, we, as an entire universe of living beings, are one. Everything in it, around it, and shaped by it is alive, always in motion, and interconnected to everything else. We know this for a fact because our common senses are designed for the sole purpose of this synergy. When the sun shines, the wind blows, or the rain falls, it brings with it the same window of life to all living beings. Nothing in the universe is spared. The human connection with the universe began in the rich cultural sangha of Afrika: the Black diaspora. Thus, Black consciousness is connected to the pulse of the universe. Black consciousness formed the first human students of the universe, and Afrikan people in America are their samsara. Black consciousness formed the first human voices and created the first human languages and the first human civilizations. Black consciousness formed the gifts of Ari, Karma, dharma, humility, and forgiveness; that we all share the same duty of preserving life; that we are all connected under the universal principle that if one living being suffers, all living beings suffer; Black consciousness formed the life lessons of compassion, mercy, pride, empathy, righteousness, courage, unity, compromise, and love; the first to apply the gift of the fourth eye. Black consciousness formed the first scholars of metaphysics, the ethnosphere, spirituality, enlightenment, and faith; the first to apply justice, under the philosophical concepts of awareness, morality, and wisdom; the first to be taught about the poisons of greed, anger, and ignorance; the first to use the family building blocks of teachers, teachings, and communities; the first to understand the law of causation, that pain and happiness, along with life and death, are all part of the interconnected cycle of life. Black consciousness formed the principles of fearlessness as a life road map; the first to recognize the duty of not contributing to evil, doing good, and doing good for others. Black consciousness is the foundational art of life (Gaskew, 2018, p. 190, 2020a,b; Williams, 2000, 2016). Yongho Nichodemus (2013) reminds us in *Theory of African Metaphysics* that the Afrikan universe sits at the center of understanding and interpreting the life and death. The Black diaspora is organic in nature, constantly in motion, connecting, manipulating, and interacting with all the life forces, which morphs into what we know as the Black consciousness.

As Pan-Afrikan people, we need to stop lying to ourselves. We don't have either a good or bad relationship with the police. We simply don't have a relationship. Policing is not part of the organic connective bond that living beings have within the universe. Policing does not recognize the cultural legacy of the first humans on the planet. The actors whose livelihood depends on policing do not recognize their duty to not spread evil, to do good, and to do good for others. Its inner core is based on the foundational poisons of greed, anger, and ignorance, all directed at the dehumanization of the Black experience in America. Thus, as Pan-Afrikan people we must disown policing from our lives. The construct which started off as slave patrols, conducting stop and frisks on Black bodies for over four centuries, has never morphed into anything other than a weaponized tool of white superiority and Black inferiority. White supremacy will always be embedded within policing. The social institution of policing was made by white Americans and is controlled by white Americans, only to serve and benefit white Americans. Policing is the gatekeeper of the Great White Shark (Gaskew, 2014a, pp. 93–98), a corporately constructed twenty-four hours a day, seven days a week eating machine and multitrillion-dollar-a-year business with the sole purpose of morally destroying Black bodies, Black culture, and Black potential. The institution of policing will never willingly surrender its cultural and political influence to inflict systemic pain and suffering against Black spaces. Its political influence must be weakened and its culture humbled (Gaskew, 2018, pp. 187–199).

Black consciousness will unfriend policing and provide a platform that will filter, deconstruct, and eliminate the by-products of shame, self-segregation, and transgenerational learned helplessness inherited by 400 years of white supremacy (Gaskew, 2018, 2020a,b). It will liberate Black spaces in the ideological war against white domination (Amos, 2014). It will produce a cultural fearlessness that challenges the legitimacy of any construct in America that attempts to criminalize Blackness. It will confront the systemic actors of direct and structural violence that use the mask of law and order to conspire against the Black diaspora. As the founders of humanity, Black people must take responsibility for their own liberation. Black consciousness makes peace with our historical legacy. Black consciousness is the vessel for decolonizing the state narrative.

Chapter 3

Decolonizing the State Narrative

Policing is just a hustle. That's what my dad always told me. Not fooling anyone are they? Study the hustle. Learn how to exploit the hustle, but train your mind, body, and soul not to trust the hustle. Master the strengths and weaknesses of the hustle and use that knowledge to educate your people. This sacrifice will be the greatest gift you can give to your people.

MONEY, MYTHS, AND MISCREANTS

Policing has always been the gatekeeper of white supremacy in America. If you were to ever take the time to peel back the layers of money, myths, and miscreants used as the face of this chattel institution over the past 330 years, you would find that policing has never tried to hide their loyalty and dedication to the white consumers of their product. Policing is proud of being the face and serving the political and cultural interests of white America. Policing, by way of its cultural DNA, has never tried to escape this truth. However, what Black people in America must understand is the more you peel back the layers, the more you begin to uncover just how fragile, weak, and vulnerable the policing culture is today. Decolonizing the state narrative is our next ritual in police abolition.

Decolonizing the state narrative, as with any process of liberation, must start with and be grounded in truth. According to *Howell Henry* (1914) in *The Police Control of the Slave in South Carolina*, Norrece Jones (1989) in *Born a Child of Freedom, Yet a Slave: Mechanisms of Control and Strategies of Resistance in Antebellum South Carolina*, Bradley Nicholson (1994) in *Legal Borrowing and the Origins of Slave Law in the British Colonies*, and Sally Hadden (2001) in *Slave Patrols: Law and Violence in Virginia and the*

Carolinas, the origins of American policing can be found in the Barbados Slave Code of 1661. The Barbados Slave Code created a legal mechanism for whites in the Caribbean to have full legal capacity to control enslaved Black people, which included the creation and use of what is commonly referred to as "slave patrols." But let's be very clear, *slave patrols* are the police. No amount of feel-good code-switching changes that fact. The Barbados Slave Codes quickly spread from the Caribbean Islands to South Carolina, where they became the legal basis for the treatment of enslaved Black people in many of the thirteen colonies and the creation of American policing. Beginning in 1704, South Carolina officially implemented a policing system, based solely on Barbadian police models.

Cumulatively, the *Negro Act of 1740, Article IV, Section 2, Clause 3 of the U.S. Constitution,* also known as *the Fugitive Slave Clause 1787, the Fugitive Slave Act of 1793*, and *Fugitive Slave Act of 1850,* all solidified the enforcement powers of American policing (Nicholson, 1994; Hadden, 2001). Thus, American policing spread from state to state. American policing became the primary mechanism used to enforce white superiority and Black inferiority. American policing became the primary mechanism used to deny enslaved Black people their universal right to life. American policing became the primary mechanism used to deny enslaved Black people their universal right of self-defense. American policing became the primary mechanism of white supremacy, mutilating and murdering tens of thousands of enslaved Black people, without fear of reprisal. These are the origins of stop and frisk, zero tolerance, broken windows, community policing, and mass incarceration. These are the origins of American policing, without debate.

Next, the history of the British role in the American policing must be exposed. According to David Olusoga (2015) in *The History of British Slave Ownership Has Been Buried: Now Its Scale Can Be Revealed,* tens of thousands of British families grew rich off the genocide of Black people, specifically from the production of sugar and cotton in the seventeenth and eighteenth centuries. Direct and indirect profits fueled the Industrial Revolution, where the accumulated wealth led to a boom in the banking industry. This is where we can find the mythical police figure known to every police officer, police cadet, and police chief in America: *Robert Peel.* Arguably, every police academy and executive police leadership school in the country hail the origins of American policing to Peel, who is described as the "father of modern policing." Robert Peel, under the Metropolitan Police Act of 1829, established the London Metropolitan Police Force, considered the model of professional policing (Siegal & Worrall, 2019). Peel is also credited with developing the *Peelian Principles,* a set of nine ethical standards that serve as the moral foundation for American policing today, declaring, "The police are the public and the public are the police" (FBI Law Enforcement Bulletin, 2011; Law Enforcement Action Partnership, 2019). Just to be clear, almost every post-secondary criminal justice and criminology program and professor in the country, along with thousands of books, book chapters, journal articles, encyclopedia entries, and technical reports, has supported and spread these same mythical police state narratives for almost two centuries.

The truth of the matter is that Robert Peel was more like the Christopher Columbus of policing. The "father of modern policing" was from a wealthy white family that directly profited from the cotton industry and the enslavement of Black people in Britain. In fact, Peel's father, raising a legal petition, vehemently opposed the *Foreign Slave Trade Abolition Bill*, which would have prevented the importation of enslaved Black people by British traders into territories belonging to foreign powers, seeing it as a threat to the cotton industry and the capital of their Black property (United Kingdom Parliament Archives, 2019). Peel later carried out his first experiments in "professional policing" supporting the colonization efforts in Ireland, by establishing the *Peace Preservation Act of 1814*, which was specifically designed to create armed forces aimed to suppress any Irish political decent. After a wave of ethnic cleansing violence against the Irish, Peel returned to Britain, setting his sights on establishing a similar but more organized version of police violence. However, Peel's impact would be felt for the next 100 years in Ireland, when his offshoot, the Royal Irish Constabulary, or what is commonly known as the *Black and Tans*, was established. The Black and Tans (aka British paramilitary police forces) committed ethnic atrocities across Ireland from 1920 to 1922, ushering in massive support for the IRA's revolutionary mantra for years to come (Bennet, 2011; National Museum of Ireland, 2019).

It is to be understood that Peel never created the so-called *Peelian* principles of policing. According to the Government of the United Kingdom (2012) *Freedom of Information Release: Definition of Policing by Consent*, there is absolutely no evidence to support, nor has there ever been of, any link to these principles to Robert Peel. Peel did not create these ethical principles of policing, and given his history, this should not come as any surprise. Just imagine, this Peelian myth has been spread by the entire policing community, including countless scholars, professors, and police practitioners in America for nearly two centuries. Evidence suggests that these principles were most likely created by the first Commissioners of Police of the Metropolis, Charles Rowan and Richard Mayne. Why does policing continue to spread these self-serving lies and myths? Money.

According to Kate Hamaji and Kumar Rao (2017) in the report *Freedom to Thrive: Reimagining Safety & Security in Our Communities*, over $100 billion is annually spent on policing in America. The City of Oakland leads the nation percentage wise, spending over 42 percent of its general allocated annual budget on policing. To place this into better context, the NYPD has an annual budget that exceeds $6 billion (The Council of the City of New York, 2019). At the end of fiscal year 2016, the market value of the endowment funds of all colleges and universities in America was $542 billion (U.S. Department of Education, 2019). NYPD's annual budget would place it as the sixteenth highest college endowment in the country. In fact, NYPD's annual budget is larger than the endowment of the University of Pittsburgh (#26 at $3.9 billion), my current employer. Endowment funds of the 120 degree-granting postsecondary institutions with the largest endowments are all primary white institutions (PWIs). Not a single Historically Black College and University (HBCU) is in the top 120. The total endowments of all HBCUs in the country does not even exceed $2.7 billion. The largest HBCU endowment belongs to Howard University, at $647 million (U.S. Department of Education, 2019). Again, just to place this into context, the combined annual budgets of the Chicago and Los Angeles police departments exceed the total sum of the endowments in all 107 HBCUs in America. Again, considering that Black faculty make up less than 5 percent of all tenure-stream faculty positions in the academic discipline of criminal justice/criminology across the country, there was very little or no scholarly pushback on these policing myths and lies. Absolutely none. This is where the dialogue of decolonizing the state narrative must begin.

WHITE LOGIC-WHITE METHODS

If the FBI told you that approximately 75 percent of all homicides in the United States are committed by someone known to the victim, would you question the data? If FBI told you that the remaining 25 percent of homicides in America were committed by a complete stranger to the victim, would you question the data? But if I told you that one-third of all stranger-generated homicides in the United States were perpetrated by the police officers, would you question the data (Ball, 2019)? In my experience, one of the most difficult constructs to decolonize is the zombie-like trust and addiction to use *white logic*—statistical data that is generated by policing or one of their *anglo-conformists, assimilados*, or emissaries sent by white society (Ture, 1967, pp. 12, 30)—as a representation of Afrikan reality in America. Ture (1967) argued:

> By speaking of logic, we refer to both the foundation of the techniques used in analyzing empirical reality, and the reasoning used by researchers in their efforts to understand society. White logic, then, refers to a context in which white supremacy has defined the techniques and processes of reasoning about social facts. (p.17)

That is, any and all logic and methodologically driven data created by the policing culture is only designed to further a systemic white agenda, regardless of who, what, when, where, why and how the data was created or is being utilized at the moment. Even if the data is critical of policing actions or behavior, it is only temporary, and there is always an invisible layer or inter-pretation of the data that will be exploited to empower white supremacy. As a word of caution, never build a police abolitionist foundation on white logic.

Tikufu Zuberi and Eduardo Bonilla-Silva (2008) offer one of the most nuanced explanations of how white logic has corrupted the methodologi-cal framing of data, in their work *White Logic, White Methods: Racism and Methodology*. Within this framework, decolonizing the state narrative requires delegitimizing the manner in which data is collected and interpreted within the social sciences. Remember, the social sciences were developed as part of the eugenics movement. This fact is undeniable. Moreover, the founder of statistical analysis also developed a theory of white supremacy, in order to explain the racial inferiority of colonial and second-class citizens in the new imperial era. *White logic* and *white methods* become very simple to understand once you expose its invisible histories under these conditions.

First, since whites in the United States are the numerical demographic majority, by design, they have created a warped racial stratification system that elevates their status and thus have an unwavering commitment at main-taining institutions of white supremacy. Second, white researchers, who by design are the overwhelming majority of American criminologists, have always aided in the development of sustaining racial stratification as a sci-entifically legitimate and socially accepted concept of understanding crime. White criminologists have an unwavering commitment at maintaining institu-tions of white supremacy. White supremacy shapes a researcher's scientific gaze, past, present, and future. Described as the father of criminology, Cesare Lombroso (1876) in *Criminal Man* advocated a eugenics approach to exam-ining the sociopolitical construct of crime. Lombroso concluded that Black people were genetically inferior and were born criminals, opening Pandora's box for the white logic scientifically based criminalization of the Black dias-pora. Lombroso's methodology continues to live and breathe in the cultural DNA of the entire academic field of criminology, hidden in plain sight within the academic pedigree of every white researcher, social scientist, or professor who calls themselves a criminologist.

Books such as *The Negro a Beast* by Charles Carroll (1900) and *Race Traits and Tendencies of the American Negro* by Frederick Hoffman's (1896) provided a Christian biblical layer of white logic, arguing that Black people in America were not human and were more akin to apes. That because of genetic inferiority, whites were vastly superior to Black people, and that due to this mythical genetic inferiority, Black people would eventually just die off. Such theoretical concepts dominated the late nineteenth- and early twentieth-century literature and gave rise to the racist eugenics' movement. Countless white researchers, social scientist, and professors in America,

including members of the University of Chicago's School of Criminology—
widely considered as the most influential criminological think tank in the
nation—embraced Lombroso's white supremacist concepts and reproduced
their own research supporting this race-based dogma. This included August
Vollmer, who is considered as the "father of American policing." Vollmer
became the first *police professor* in the United States, when he was appointed
to the faculty of the University of Chicago in 1929. During his tenure,
Vollmer worked with the International Association of Chiefs of Police
(IACP) in the establishment of the UCR (Oliver, 2019). More on the UCR
later in this chapter. With the exception of the amazing work of Dubois and
a handful of other intellectuals within the Black diaspora, white researchers,
social scientists, and university professors were unchallenged to saturate
courses, publications, doctoral studies programs, and conference presentations with research findings that supported their own white logic and their
own white scientific gaze.

Third, even after the integration of a few Black scholars, criminology
remained numerically, logically, and methodologically a discipline structured
by whites to support their whiteness. Criminology and criminal justice have
always been and will always be academic disciplines that are whitewashed.
White logic and white methods are the dogma of criminal justice and criminology research. This has led to a criminological white-man's burden and the
urge for white criminologists to educate and civilize us *Black intellectuals*
in America on our role within the academic discipline. In the spirit of my
intellectual ancestors within the Black diaspora, it is with great pride and
enthusiasm that I publicly challenge and reject everything that comes out of
the mouth or pen of any white researcher, social scientist, or professor, who
claims to explain the Black experience in America. The knowledge and experience basis of whites, as a group, leads them to produce racial knowledge
that tends to reproduce their self-created racial order. White methods are the
practical tools used to manufacture empirical data and analysis to support
a white supremacist agenda. Albert Murray (1973) in *The Death of White
Sociology* noted:

> There is little reason why Negroes should not regard contemporary social
> science theory and techniques with anything except the most unrelenting
> suspicion. There is, come to think of it, no truly compelling reason at all why
> Negroes should not regard the use of the social science statistical survey as the
> most elaborate fraud of modern times. In any event, they should never forget
> that the group in power is always likely to use every means at its disposal to
> create the impression that it deserves to be where it is. And it is not above sug-
> gesting that those who have been excluded have only themselves to blame. (pp.
> 96–112)

The academy became an important, and in many ways still is, perfect weapon of white supremacy in America. Liberalism is only a mask for white supremacy. J. Edgar Hoover and the FBI were closely listening and learning.

WHITE LOGIC-WHITE DATA

One of the most difficult state narratives on policing to decolonize is hidden within the myths of the UCR, the NIBRS, and the NCVS. Simply put, the UCR, NIBRS, and NCVS are policing tools used to continue the criminalization of the Black narrative. Please do not try and overthink this issue. They are used as weapons against the Black diaspora. The UCR, NIBRS, and NCVS do not measure the construct of crime. The UCR, NIBRS, and NCVS measure the construct of police activity. There is a huge intellectual difference between the two. The UCR, NIBRS, and NCVS measure how police agencies interpret and respond to the construct of crime based on racial stratifications. All of this data contains reporting errors, is unreliable, unverifiable, untimely, and incomplete, and intentionally misreports, under-reports, and over-reports how police interpret the construct of crime, again, within a warped racial stratification system. In fact, the FBI creates estimates on any missing data. For nearly ninety years, the UCR did not even track the sexual assaults of men in the United States. Imagine the millions of Black males who became victims of sexual assault through the hands of stop and frisk in America. The UCR, NIBRS, and NCVS measure the depths of policing involvement in the racial, economic, political, and cultural warfare sustained on the globe's aboriginal population in America (Gaskew, 2014a, 2018).

The UCR is considered the oldest extant national crime data system in the United States, with the possible exception of some prison statistics. The UCR continues to be the most believed and widely accepted crime data system in America, because of its extensive exception and use by scholars, social critics, governmental organizations, and media around the country, and as such, no other database in existence has shaped how the world frames the Black diaspora in America. You see, prior to the creation of the UCR, the only data instrument available to measure the impact of "post-slavery" on the Black diaspora was the publication of the 1890 US Census. It is to be understood that the American Civil War, the Progressive Era, and the Reconstruction Era witnessed renewed efforts to enslave Black people under a new property owner: the US government.

The 1890 US Census set the stage for using racial stratification as government-sanctioned social capital, adding a racial identifier to its questionnaire. The question placed "Japanese" as a category for the first time, along with "Chinese," "Negro," "mulatto," "quadroon," "octoroon," and "white" (United

States Census Bureau, 2019). Under the umbrella of twenty-five years of the discriminatory Black Codes, the Census report suggested that although Black people in America made up less than 12 percent of the total population, 30 percent of America's prison population consisted of Black men (Muhammad, 2010). It is no coincidence that the US government established its own federal prison system in 1891, soon after the release of the 1890 US Census report. The Three Prisons Act established funding for Ft. Leavenworth, McNeil Island, and UPS Atlanta (Federal Bureau of Prisons, 2019), setting the stage for a weaponized future where today, over 120 federal prisons are spread across rural white America, employing nearly 25,000 white people, all profiting from the government's war on Black bodies.

Taking this US Census data as unquestionable fact and overlooking the race-based motivations of white researchers, social scientists, and professors across the nation, this 1890 Census incarceration data was used to criminalize the Black diaspora while at the same time romanticizing white immigrants, in the hearts and minds of the world. Charles Henderson (1901), a sociologist from the "Chicago School" of criminological thought, published arguably the first academic textbook on crime in America, *An Introduction to the Study of the Dependent, Defective, and Delinquent Classes*, apologizing for the crimes of white immigrants while exasperating the fear of Black males. Henderson (1901) wrote:

> The Negro factor . . . racial inheritance, physical and mental inferiority, barbarian and slave ancestry and culture . . . were the most serious factors in crime statistics. (pp. 246–247)

White university professors across the nation agreed to creating an "imagined community" (Anderson, 1991) of crime, inferiority, and deviant behavior within the Black diaspora while simultaneously explaining the massive crime wave of organized crime by white immigrants as assimilating into the "American Process" (Muhammad, 2010). Have you ever wondered why the likes of white immigrants such as Carlo Gambino, Lucky Luciano, Frank Costello, Al Capone, and such were created into romanticized figures of robin hood-like mythology? The social construct of the United States formed a wall of exclusion and alienation for the Black diaspora, specifically Black males. During the infancy stages of the Black diaspora's liberation from transatlantic enslavement, when white American academicians could have sought moral, psychological, and physical refuge for their sins by promoting scholarship on creating reparations for the Afrikan Holocaust, they used the powers of the academy to frame the criminal justice system, specifically the institution of policing, to perpetuate the myths of inferiority and criminality, and to exacerbate the fear of Black existence (Gaskew, 2014a).

Capitalizing on this mythical "Black fear" under the guidance of white academicians, the Social Science Research Council, and the IACP, J. Edgar Hoover in 1930 published the nation's very first government-authorized crime data: the UCR. Hoover had been well versed in race-based policing tactics his entire career. From 1917 to 1924, Hoover was the head of DOJ's Bureau of Investigations *Alien Enemy & Intelligence Division* which surveilled, discredited, arrested, imprisoned, and deported anyone considered a domestic radical. Marcus Garvey would become one of Hoover's highest priorities, targeted for assassination, incarceration, or deportation. In 1924, the Coolidge administration appointed Hoover as the director of the Bureau of Investigations, the predecessor of what we know today as the Federal Bureau of Investigations (Rosen, 2016).

For over ninety years, the FBI has served as the data clearinghouse, organizing, collecting, and disseminating crime-based information voluntarily submitted by over 18,000 local, state, federal, and tribal law enforcement agencies across the country. This data is routinely used by politicians, police chiefs, and policy makers alike to gauge their impact in lowering crime around the nation. What Edgar did at the height of Jim Crow was to frame the construct of crime into race-based categories, making the FBI the sole "authoritative statistical gatekeeper" of crime data in America (Muhammad, 2010). Initially, the UCR had a category table labeled "Foreign Born White" to represent the crimes committed by Italian, Irish, and other immigrant Europeans; however, this category disappeared quickly as Hoover blended their crimes into the "White" category. The other categories were "Negro," "Indian," "Chinese," "Japanese," "Mexican," and all others (U.S. Department of Justice-UCR, 1930–1956). Thus, the FBI presented a "numbers speak for themselves" rationale, pitting white Americans against the Black diaspora, where the outcome was predetermined in Hoover's racist perception of America. The FBI was able to create the construct of crime and criminalize the Black diaspora, because the database was reflective of the annotated race listed on the fingerprint cards sent to their identification division by police agencies around the country. Police agencies across the country were misrepresenting the race on fingerprint cards, intentionally over-representing the Black diaspora. American policing, since its origins with the Barbadian Slave Codes, have always been active systematic provocateurs of white supremacy. Muhammad (2010) noted:

> Police misconduct, corruption, and brutality . . . helped to produce disproportionately high black arrest rates, the starting point for high juvenile delinquency commitments and adult prison rates. (p. 12)

The FBI's motivation for documenting crimes by race and/or ethnicity, as well as the credibility and reliability of the information they received and the statistics they disseminated by police departments, was never questioned by the executive, legislative, or judicial branches of the federal government because this data provided the US government what they needed in order to replace the incredible financial capital lost by the free labor of enslavement: an enemy of the state. Black people soon became synonymous with crime and a victim of the corrupt legacy of Black criminalization. Today, very similar to 1930, "race" is constructed within four UCR offender categories: (1) white; (2) Black; (3) American Indian or Alaskan Native; and (4) Native Hawaiian or Other Pacific Islander. In fact, the UCR only recently designated a special "Ethnicity" category entitled "Hispanic or Latino." For over eighty-five years, the FBI has been deceptively lumping all Latinx people arrested in the United States into the "White" category, creating a "smoke and mirrors" tactic used to make the "White" category seem larger than it is. There has never been one single positive contribution to understanding the social construct of crime by placing people into racial categories, other than to entice racial profiling and criminalize Afrikan people in America (Gaskew, 2014a).

Using data from the UCR, Edgar created specialized programs to recruit and retain Black people in America as informants, to spy on their own Black communities. With BLACPRO (Black Informant Program) and the Ghetto Informant Program, the FBI maintained over 5,000 active Black informants across the country. Hoover had informants on various HBCUs, specifically faculty, staff, and students at Florida A&M and Tennessee A&I. He used data from the UCR to establish informants in every Black organization, including the NAACP, the NOI, USA, the BPP, the Student Nonviolent Coordinating Committee, as well as within Martin Luther King's and Malcolm X's inner circles. In fact, it could be argued that the Black diaspora in America has never recovered from the effects of FBI's informant counterintelligence programs (Gaskew, 2014a). Loyalty, trust, connectivity, synergy, safety, and cultural and spiritual heritage, all attributes of a healthy community, were taken and replaced with disloyalty, untruth, dependence, selfishness, and historical amnesia. Despite an intense rivalry between the FBI and the Central Intelligence Agency (CIA), Hoover solicited covert information on "racial matters intelligence" from the CIA under operations "Project Hunter," "CHAOS," and "RESISTANCE." In Project Hunter, the CIA along with the FBI opened, read, and photographed over 100,000 letters from American citizens, including those of Martin Luther King's wife Coretta. CHAOS focused on the foreign relationship between Black social movements and the NOI. RESISTANCE placed an emphasis on the relationship between communism and Black social movements (Blackstock, 1988; Davis, 1992; Gaskew, 2014a, O'Reilly, 1990).

Remember, COINTELPRO prototypes, including BLACPRO, date back over 100 years, and there is growing evidence that suggests the UCR used today originated as part of these early operations. Most people do not realize that Hoover already had forty-five years of COINTELPRO operational field work experience (unlawful human and electronic intelligence) before he unleashed its violence on the Black Power Movement (Gaskew, 2014a).

The NIBRS and the NCVS are no different. NIBRS was established at the height of the Reagan administration's ongoing war on drugs in 1985, by way of an FBI report entitled "Blueprint for the Future of the Uniform Crime Reporting Program" (FBI, 2019). Similar to the UCR, NIBRS is a criminal database system that is under the complete control of the FBI, which speaks for itself. In addition, similar to the UCR, NIBRS is created from voluntarily and selectively constructed crime data by police departments from across the country. Every single piece of data in NIBRS could have been falsified or manipulated by the participating self-reporting police agencies or the FBI. Again, policing can never be trusted to provide reliable data regarding the Black diaspora in America. Never.

The NCVS was officially established in 1972 under J. Edgar Hoover and the Nixon administration's war on drugs, as a by-product of the Johnson administration's formation of *The Presidents Commission on Law Enforcement and Administration of Justice* (1967) and the commission's subsequent report "The Challenge of Crime in a Free Society." The same Lyndon B. Johnson who gave J. Edgar a complete free hand to implement the FBI's destructive COINTELPRO aimed directly at the Black diaspora and its leadership. The same Lyndon B. Johnson who received daily intelligence briefings on COINTELPRO's unlawful activities. Yes, the same Lyndon B. Johnson who regularly referred to Black people in America as "niggers" (Kessler, 2017). This is the Richard Nixon who used COINTELPRO to declare war on the BPP and carried out the assassination of Fred Hampton. The president's commission recommended four areas for police reform, all of which became future weapons of mass destruction, aimed directly at the Black diaspora across the country:

- Ongoing financial incentives to support police training (military grade weaponry and tactics).
- The development of Community Oriented Policing (stop & frisk).
- Ongoing federal funding for police directed crime initiatives (zero tolerance and the war on drugs).
- The creation of the National Crime Victimization Survey (data used to racially criminalize). (pp. v-vi)

According to the Bureau of Justice Statistics (2019) report, "Data Collection: National Crime Victimization Survey," the NCVS is the nation's primary source of information on criminal victimization. Its methodology is based on using a sample size of about 240,000 voluntary interviews, involving 160,000 persons in about 95,000 households. According to the report, the US Census Bureau chooses the voluntary participants by randomly selecting addresses across the country. Each household occupant over the age of twelve acts as volunteer survey participants. The survey focuses on gathering information on the following constructed incidents: assault, burglary, larceny, motor vehicle theft, rape, and robbery. The survey results are then used to create a crime index database. Bureau of Justice Statistics (2019) stipulate that survey respondents provide demographic information about themselves and the alleged actors (age, sex, race, ethnicity, marital status, education level, income, and the victim offender relationship), characteristics of the incident (time and place of incident, use of weapons, nature of injury, and economic consequences), whether the incident was reported to police, reasons the incident was or was not reported, and victim experiences with the criminal justice system (BJS, 2019).

As with the UCR and the NIBRS, the NCVS relies on the virtue of the Black diaspora's blind trust. Blind trust that the sampling protocol and survey methodology, established by the US government, are credible, reliable, and accurate. Blind trust that the data collector performing the interview (government employee) is truthful. Blind trust that this same data collector does not interject any racial bias, during their interpersonal interaction with the participants, that will impact the findings. Blind trust that the results of this survey will not be used to criminalize the Black experience in America. Not a chance. For example, according to one of the latest Bureau of Justice Statistics (2017) NCVS data reports, "Race and Hispanic Origin of Victims and Offenders, 2012–15," over 5.8 million victimizations took place in the United States during this time period. Although white Americans are roughly 76 percent of the population and the Black diaspora nearly 13 percent of the US population, the report indicates that less than 43 percent of the victimization offenders were white, but a disproportional high 23 percent of the offenders were identified by the survey participants as Black. Keep in mind, prior to 2012, the NCVS offender race categories were only "White," "Black," or "Other." Only in 2012 did the government begin to add categories that included "American Indian," "Alaska Native," "Asian," "Native Hawaiian," "Other Pacific Islander," and the ethnicity of "Hispanic." Smoke and mirrors again. Sound familiar? In fact, there is absolutely no mechanism to verify whether the victim-offender demographic information provided by survey participants is accurate, reliable, or trustworthy.

In the end, countless police profiteers, researchers, social scientists, and university professors white-washed data, and continue to, in order to serve their own interests and the interests of white supremacy. Understanding the entire systemic process of criminalization can be a useful weapon of decolonization within the police abolition revolution. Knowing that there are grassroots abolitionist organizations around the country that are already putting this theory into practice provides another layer of dismantling the states narrative on policing.

ABOLITION ORGANIZATIONAL SPACES

Remember, decolonizing the state narrative is only one tactic in the revolutionary process of police abolition. The reality is that there are several grassroots abolition organizations in America that have already effectively implemented a decolonizing narrative in cities across the country, placing theory into practice. Some of these abolition organizations work diligently to empower communities to peel back the money, myths, and miscreants of policing, in order to expose the fragility, weaknesses, and vulnerabilities the policing culture lives with today. However, just as a cautionary voice, although my conversations with abolitionists and their supporters across America helped to construct my understanding of the nuanced approaches used by these movements and how they levy their grassroots influence to compel policy initiatives that have opened the door for police abolition initiatives, I was always reminded of the words of the Black Liberation Army (1971):

> We are not afraid of white people controlling our movement, for our formations, guns, and ideas are built with our own hands, efforts, and blood. The BLA supports [tactical] alliances with whites if it meant benefiting the Black race. (pp. iv–5)

My conversations with abolitionists also demonstrated to me how white supremacy permeates these movements as well. CRT applies to abolitionism in America. CRT lives in abolition movements across the country. As already noted, a significant amount of abolitionism energy is expended by keeping its white liberal membership, white liberal allies, and white liberal funding organizations happy. The power dynamics is grossly skewed towards catering to the desires of white liberals. Pathological pacifism (Churchill, 2007) has given birth to what I call the gentrification of abolitionism. At the end of the day, for some white abolitionists, it's still about how to maintain their own power, control, and influence over the aboriginal Black diaspora. Often, lost in this sea of white liberalism is the goal of Black self-determinism, Black power, and Black liberation. Secondly, I discovered there is a significant difference between police abolition actors and prison abolition actors, within the same white liberal abolition spaces. Again, that's another conversation for another book. Although several abolition organizations offer sound tactics, as I note throughout my book, and as the Black Liberation Army (1971) highlights, ultimately a progressive liberal tactic that rejects revolution will never result in dismantling American policing. Ultimately, I discovered that it was not in the best interest of some abolition organizations to dismantle the institution of policing (Gaskew, 2014a,b, 2018, 2020a). However, I'd like to highlight a few grassroots abolition spaces whose tactical approach to challenging the states narrative of policing stood out.

A World Without Police (2019, para. 1–3) developed a comprehensive strategy aimed toward creating a holistic approach to significantly rolling back policing powers and finding alternatives to policing in America. Separated into three collective parts, *Disempower, Disarm, and Disband*, the strategy includes a detailed study guide, which is separated into seven sections: *The Creation of Police Forces*; *The Police Role in Capitalist Society*; *White Supremacy and Class Rule*; *Policing Gender*; *"Blue Power" and Police Unions*; *Community Policing and Repression*; and *Toward Abolition*. The guide is intended to help activists understand policing and craft strategies to limit their power and impact, by examining the role police play in modern society and how they came to serve this function. In addition, it explores the impacts and contradictions of policing and closes with a look at how communities have resisted police impunity and created alternative means of public safety. *A World Without Police* (2019) recommends reviewing this study with friends, comrades, and others directly impacted by policing and prisons: each one, teach one (para. 1–3).

MPD150 (2019b) provides a unique approach for shifting the power narrative of how policing, crime, and safety are understood. MPD150 produced a participatory action report entitled "Enough is Enough," which is a 150-year performance review of the Minneapolis Police Department (MPD). This report is the product of an exhaustive investigation into the conduct of the Minneapolis Police Department over the fifteen decades since its founding in 1867. The report includes a survey of its current role and impact, especially on marginalized communities, and an exploration of viable alternatives to the policing model. "Enough is Enough" is the type of initiative every community in the United States should be conducting on police agencies.

According to the *Stop Police Terror Project DC* (2019b, para. 1), "The greatest tool in battling systemic issues of police violence is to arm ourselves with knowledge and to band together as a community." SPTP (2019b) created a *Get Informed* web-link where a plethora of research material on policing and the Metropolitan Police Department can be located.

Baltimore Bloc (2019), a grassroots collective of friends, families, and neighborhoods united to rebuild communities and organize for *kujichagulia*, provides a much more direct platform for decolonizing the state narrative of policing. Baltimore Bloc actively post the photographs and included information on Baltimore City Police Department officers who have been publicly identified in police misconduct violation. The website currently displays the photos and related information on ten police officers, including the recent former Commissioner of BPD, Darryl De Sousa, who was sentenced to ten months in federal prison in 2019 for federal tax-related crimes.

Critical Resistance (2019a) provides an *Abolition of Policing Workshop*, which applies a multifaceted empirical overview of policing in America, chronicling a historical assessment from its origins as slave patrols, to the continued role policing plays as agents of oppression, enforcing Trump's brand of white supremacy across the nation today. This online workshop platform is a one-stop-shop for decolonizing the states narrative on policing, using evidence-based data, facilitator training, alternative justice systems, scenario-building exercises, and a variety of scholarly publications that push the creative boundaries of decolonization, such as *Standing Up for Our Communities: Why We Need a Police-Free Future*, *Big Dreams and Bold Steps Toward a Police-Free Future*, and *The Oakland Power Projects.*

One of the greatest tools for dismantling systemic policing in America is to weaponize Black intellectualism and to organize the collective gifts of the Black diaspora. This chapter emphasizes the power of decolonizing Black intellectual spaces from data, statistics, or any propaganda that serves the interests of white supremacy. Once the Black diaspora has decolonized itself from the myths, miscreants, and money that fuel the police propaganda machine in America, the next revolutionary ritual in the process of police abolition becomes universally clear: community self-determination.

Chapter 4

Community Self-Determination

We were living in the Harold Icky Housing Projects. I think I was six years old at the time. My mom was walking me to school, and a few neighborhood guys who were standing in the corridor of the apartment mumbled something toward us as we walked by. I couldn't hear what they said, but they exchanged some words with my mom and she was visibly not happy. My mom immediately returned to our apartment, where she told my dad what had happened. A few minutes later, several men entered our apartment that I did not recognize. They all left together in a hurry. I never saw those guys standing in the corridor again. There were rumors. Sometimes your survival in a community depends on learning to make the right enemies.

A PAN-AFRIKAN CONSTRUCT OF COMMUNITY

Marcus Garvey's (1927) *The Tragedy of White Injustice* sets an empirical tone immersed in the cultural, political, and spiritual requirements of Pan-Afrikan self-determinism, as a prerequisite to Black liberation. In fact, an argument could be made that there would be no El Hajj Malik El Shabazz, Kwame Ture, Robert F. Williams, Huey Newton, Jamil Al-Amin, Assata Shakur, or Jalil Muntaqim without Garvey's prophetic analysis of Blackness in America. The theoretical and practical arguments for the Black diaspora's self-determination against the institution of American policing sit at the fundamental core for Black liberation. The Black Liberation Army (1971) noted:

> We as Blacks in North America, must realize that to seek inclusion into the prevailing system is suicide in the long run . . . our first obligation is to ourselves, this means our first obligation is to secure our total liberation from these forces

57

[policing] that maintain our oppressive condition. Related to this self-obligation, is our obligation to all oppressed peoples throughout the world, for in striving to liberate ourselves we must abolish a system that enslaves others throughout the world. This, in essence, is our historic duty. That we must strive for the abolishment of these systems . . . in which Black people have total and absolute control over their own destiny as a people. That is, in order to abolish our systems of oppression, we must utilize the science of [revolution] and develop this science as it relates to our unique national condition. (pp. 8–9)

American policing will never understand the communal dimensions of Pan-Afrikan self-determination in America. According to Fu-Kiau Bunseki (2001), in *African Cosmology of the Bantu-Kongo: Tying the Spiritual Knot, Principles of Life & Living*, the power of justice must lie within the *kanda* or community. That there is no fundamental need for policing in an Afrikan-centered community because the community and the individual are one. Black communities are like forests. A forest with one type of tree is not a forest, for a forest is made from a unique set of different tree-life that creates a forest. Our Black cultural, linguistic, artistic, spiritual, and cosmological life is the basis of our forest. The Black diaspora is a collectivist and self-determined culture. The true nature of white supremacy does not have the depth to understand this fact. Afrikan people have a cosmological tie to one another, as the aboriginal community of mankind. That is, when one member of the Black community suffers, the community as a whole suffers. This is based on the foundational belief that community is centered on *Kimuntu*—the self-determined state of being human. Policing in America has less to do with humanity and more to do with "no-soul-minded objects" and exploitation (Bunseki, 2001, p. 50). Black community self-determination leads to police abolition.

Buneski (2001) argues that the Black diaspora lives through a set of community-based proverbs. These proverbs spell out the ritual of self-determination and are contrary to the narrative of what policing in America has spread about the Pan-Afrikan community. These Afrikan proverbs reinforce and serve as reminder that policing in America will never be part of the Black community:

• The community did exist before you; the community leads everything, for it is the head.
• The community solves community problems.
• The community is responsible for creating and enforcing laws for its members.
• To know the community is to know their cosmological connection to the universe.

- The natural principle of change transmits itself perpetually in us through the community continuum.
- Natural laws are irreversible.
- Within the community everybody has the right to teach and be taught. Education is a matter of reciprocity.
- What belongs to the community belongs to the nation.
- The community is not built outside of its social system.
- The community is a channel; people go (die), people come (are born).
- Societal leaders move and act through the masses.
- The community names you. Try to live up to what the community expects or you.
- The community members only are able to do what a stranger cannot do for its safety as well as for its human being. No one can do better than yourself.
- When the community leadership loses its direction, the community is oppressed.
- Community members are born simple, nice, and good, but they become what the community wants them to be/become. The actual behavior of a human being is a learned behavior. Very often one's nature is oppressed by the society.
- The community is taboo: never can one throw it away, and never can one own it.
- The community took care of me; I will take care of that community. Community life is a process of receiving and transmitting/passing on.
- I do not choose my community; it is the community that chooses me by giving birth to me/by brining me where I am.
- The presence of a female in a community is the symbol of a continuity of life in that community, and on the contrary, her absence is a symbol of its end. The feminine life (God) in and round us.
- The common and public house is the symbol of an alive community.
- The community is at the same time poison and honey. The community is very sticky to its members.
- The community is the union of the ancestors and of living people.
- There are no boundaries of land within community land. Ownership is public, for no one came into the world with a piece of land in his/her hand. Therefore, it cannot be sold, bought, or alienated.
- If you curse the community, you curse yourself.
- If you do leave the principles of the community system, you become an errant and a deviant.
- If the concept of community is annihilated/destroyed, the world is destroyed.
- The wisdom of the community prophesizes. The community sees farther than an individual can.

- The real wisdom of a society and its very basic needs are only known by those who mingle within the reality of people daily lives in that society.
- The community welcomes all human beings as long as they do not dare to interfere with its basic social practices/principle.
- Do not destroy the reputation of the community while wearing, somewhere else, the label of being a stranger. Your misconduct, elsewhere, has direct or indirect impact on your community as well as yourself.
- The quarrels between communities are solved by diplomatic encounters. The diplomacy (*kimawubi*) is the key to peace.
- Tend to your affairs and let others preoccupy themselves with theirs. Try to learn thoroughly what is going on in your own society before probing other societies.
- Today we are community members; tomorrow we will be the ancestors of the community.
- The community is a place of joy, love, and life.
- Social conflicts within the community are less harmful than exile.
- If the community lacks the land, the door for survival, its members will disperse.
- Human community always has problems to confront. Life is a perpetual debate. To be a community member is to be ready to confront problems.
- Community issues (affairs) do not have anniversaries; they happen anytime. Anything at anytime many happen within a community.
- In worshiping one's own wealth, one loses rights and enjoyment of his/her community. Shared wealth leads to happiness.
- Community plans/projects are an infant in their mother's womb, they are without a name. If the name of your plan explicitly tells you what you want to do, don't tell it to your enemy. Keep it secret (code it . . . *kanga yo kolo*)
- Our present knowledge in ways of coding and decoding cultural codes of alien cultures is the cornerstone in human antagonism in the world today.
- The community leader is an object of critics.
- Where there is community leadership (djinn), there is the center of the community. Communities like people have a heart.
- If not by birth, one becomes a member of the community by refuge (adoption/exile).
- There are not two different laws in a community.
- The community must pay a particular attention to its youth as well as to its land, the fundamental capital of a society.
- The center (cavity) of the community is located between the above and the below world. The reality of cultural heritage of a community, i.e., its knowledge, is the experience of that deepest knowledge found between the spiritualized ancestors and the physically living thinkers within the community. (pp. 98–112)

THE PAN-AFRIKAN CONSTRUCT OF CRIME

Within a Pan-Afrikan aboriginal worldview of community, the skewed construct known as "crime" is easily exposed for its white supremacist agenda. In order to fully understand how the concept is manipulated, one must understand the differences between how white European settlers and the Pan-Afrikan culture define the concept of crime (Buneski, 2001). Within a white European cultural narrative, the individual is the primary state of one's being. The individual sits alone at the center of the universe. Nothing is greater than the self. Choice and freedom of choice are controlled by the self, and thus are individual mandates. If freedom of choice lies within the realm of the individual, and the individual chooses to commit a crime, the individual alone is responsible for this crime. The individual is either conscious or unconscious of the crime, and thus, the individual alone holds the burden for the crime (Ani, 1994). The law of causation does not exist within this realm. This skewed worldview also explains the white European perspective on punishment; that is, the individual sits at the center of the universe and has freedom of choice. Therefore, if the individual chooses to commit a crime, the individual alone must be punished. The community does not control the process of truth and justice. The state (an individualized entity) controls the process. This is the essence of white supremacy.

The Pan-Afrikan perspective on the construct of crime and punishment is much different. Within this aboriginal realm, life is an interconnective continuum of stages. When the physical body dies, the soul of that living being remains as part of that community (Buneski, 2001, p. 71). Knowledge is not an individual endeavor but a community process. Knowledge is not in us. Knowledge is outside of us (p. 72). Within the Black diaspora, the community is connected to the universe. The individual is not greater than the community. The community chooses one's purpose in life. Choice and freedom of choice are filtered through an interconnected web of social, psychological, and physiological interactions within the community. The individual receives her/his nourishment through the community, and the community receives its nourishment through its aboriginal Afrikan rituals, beliefs, and lifestyle. The community bears the burden of awakening the unconscious to the conscious (Ani, 1994). Over the past 400 years, Pan-Afrikan communities have been at war with America over our access to our ancestral nourishment. The worldviews of the Black diaspora and the construct of whiteness within American policing have always and will always be on a collision course. The law of causation and *Ari* never ceased to exist.

Within the Black diaspora in America, there are always much larger cultural, linguistic, and environmental roots to how the construct of crime is defined, framed, and applied. Crime is a synthetic construct. Crime is a learned state of mind. Crime is transmitted into a community. Crime is never an individualized process. The construct of crime is an effect, never a cause. Crime is always a reaction. The individual, before *bearing a crime*, carries a certain set of learned constructs, concepts, images, expressions, symbols, discussions, words, habits, and facts (Buneski, 2001). In America, all of these constructs have been used to criminalize Blackness and create a narrative that provides the state ownership of individual Black bodies. Crime is part of the colonized mandate that America uses to enslave Black spaces. It removes community ownership and control of truth and justice. This includes the impact of internalized metaphysical trauma brought on by many external poisons excreted from white supremacy. In Black communities, this involves the water we drink and the food we eat. The air we breathe. The words we use to describe ourselves and the vocabulary we use to communicate with others in our community. What we use to nourish our souls and the spirits of our ancestors. Even the purity of the land we live on. Within the Pan-Afrikan worldview, crimes are the synthetically constructed poisons that strip a community of its wholeness. Thus, criminals are the processes that transmit the poisons of greed, fear, and ignorance into a community. Within the Pan-Afrikan diaspora in America, white supremacy is the greatest industrializer of crime. Policing is an American industrial complex. Policing infects Black communities with crime. Policing poisons Black communities with crime. Policing is the root cause of crime within Black communities. Policing's mere presence disturbs the aboriginal balance of truth and justice.

Secondly, and more importantly, punishment is a community-controlled and community-applied process within the Pan-Afrikan diaspora. Remember, justice is not an individual; justice is a community. This perspective deals with the root causes of crime. This perspective confronts the poisons that infect a community with crime. This perspective recognizes that white supremacy is the greatest industrializer of crime. Buneski (2001) provides a proverbial message that should resonate through the fragile policing community in America and how truth and justice will be served to those who bring the poisons of crime into the Black diaspora:

> When a crime is committed, judgment should not only be passed on to the criminal [individual], but also on the entire community in which the crime found its roots. A community in which a man or a women poisons [a community] would have trouble finding new alliances within other communities and will say to such a community. As a consequence, nobody will shake hands anymore with someone from that community; nobody will politically deal with such a community; nobody will seek water in such a community; nobody will dream to marry in such a community; and nobody will seek a good friend in that community. (pp. 74–75)

The American policing community will never have a friend within the Black diaspora. Black communities across American know that white supremacy is the cause of community suffering and that policing is white supremacy. As noted in chapter 2, Black communities will condemn not just individual officers for community-wide crimes against humanity but the entire policing culture.

PAN-AFRIKAN COMMUNITY CONTROL OF POLICING

When a white liberal hears the term "community control of policing," it is immediately interpreted into the language of police reform. Civilian review boards, citizen police academies, community policing, predictive policing, body cameras, implicit bias training, procedural justice, place-based policing, and focused deterrence are some of the more common themes that immediately come to mind. None of these approaches are designed to shift policing power and control to the Black community. They are designed to shift the power of policing to white liberals. When a Black revolutionary hears the term "community control of policing," it is immediacy interpreted into the language of self-determinism. Creating community-controlled grassroots organizations that retain the sole power to hire and fire police officers, mandate the police internal affairs investigative process, determine police disciplinary action in cases of misconduct, determine the funding of police agencies, set and enforce internal department policies, and retain concrete means of retrieving information, including subpoena power, from police agencies and third parties, as it pertains to circumstances involving police misconduct, sits at the core of Black self-determinism. This approach is designed to shift all policing power and control into the revolutionary hands of the Black community. Community control of the police is one step closer to police abolition.

In 1970, the BPP published a newsletter, *Police Petition*, outlining a referendum entitled *Community Control of Police*. The BPP understood that the permanence of white supremacy and racism within the institution of policing in America required immediate and full community control over policing actions within Black spaces. The real question became *how*? Using a sociopolitical platform, the BPP created a legislative referendum that supported Ture's (1967) demand for Black power under two central themes. First, the referendum called for a trilevel body of *Community Commissioners*, duly elected by the Black community, to lead police agencies rather than settling for the appointment of a single police chief. Second, and most importantly, the referendum called for the creation of three *Community Review Boards*, consisting of at least five members, again duly elected by the Black community, with the complete power and control to investigate and discipline any and all police actions (Newton, 1972). Although the referendum lost by less than one percentage point, it provided a future blueprint for developing community self-determinism over policing, as a prerequisite for abolishment.

In every practical sense, community control over policing is a prerequisite to abolishing the institution of American policing. That is, you can do whatever you want to an entity that you control and have ownership over. It is the essence of self-determinism. The institution of policing is no exception. You can strip policing of its military weapons. You can strip policing of its pension protections. You can break up drug and intelligence units. You can dismantle the application of the use of force standards and qualified immunity. You can require police officers carry individual insurance liability. You can defund policing if you wish. However, we must recognize and acknowledge the severe limitations of using legislative platforms as tools for Black liberation. Americans liberal legislative fairy tales are a direct by-product of white supremacy and fall under the narrative of CRT in its racially oppressive permanence. Thus, legislative interventions must be crafted carefully and understood as only initial steps in the abolishing process.

M Adams and Max Rameau (2016), in *Black Community Control Over Police*, emphasized that shifting the power of policing into the hands of the Black community is a fundamental core principle in the evolution to Black liberation.

> From a visionary standpoint, it ultimately is to self-determine what is and how to do safety in our community. That is to say, the only way the police can represent and enforce the interests of the Black community—rather than the interests of outside colonial forces oppressing and exploiting the Black community—is for the Black community to exercise complete control over the police. Efforts to reform a colonial system are futile. (pp. 519–529)

Adams and Rameau (2016) noted that community control over police is a significant step toward Black self-determination and a significant shift to end the colonial occupation between the state and the Black diaspora. This shift must manifest in the form of Civilian Police Control Board (CPCB) composed of Black residents subject to the police jurisdiction, with 100 percent complete authority over the priorities, policies, and practices of the police.

> To be perfectly clear, this is not a call for some type of civilian investigative, oversight, or review board. With full control over the police, civilian review is redundant and unnecessary. This is not a call for more community policing, where the police know each of the family members of the person they are arresting and will use those relationships to gather information for the purpose

of placing more people behind bars. This is a call for *Community Control Over Police* as a means of shifting power . . . deconstructing the historic relationship between the police and the Black community, and re-imagining a social force designed to actually protect and serve its population as policy, not as a meaningless slogan developed by a PR department. There is no purpose or dignity, in reforming a colonial relationship. The only option is to end that relationship. The only way to end police terror against low-income Black communities is to permanently end the colonial relationship between those communities and the police departments that serve as occupying forces. (p. 539)

According to Diop Olugbala (2019) in *Black is Back Coalition: Black Community Control of Police in Philly,* an initiative that mandates community control over policing is long overdue. They suggest as an act of Black self-determinism, creating a commission independent of the state/government, elected by the residents within Black community police districts, to control policing in their respective neighborhoods. This commission would function to *police the police* and to liberate the Black community by first dismantling the Fraternal Order of Police (FOP). This initiative serves as part of the *Black is Back Coalition of Social Justice, Peace, and Reparations* (2019, para. 1) 19-point mandate, which includes an end to the police containment of Afrikan people within America.

The Chicago Alliance against Racist and Political Repression (2018), together with representatives of several Pan-Afrikan grassroots organizations across Chicago, created proposed legislation that establishes a sociopolitical platform for community control over policing and community-based justice systems: *Civilian Police Accountability Council* (CPAC). The legislation provides complete and total community-based control over policing in Chicago. If approved, CPAC (2018) will have the power to

- Appoint the Superintendent of Police.
- Re-write the police rule book, including all use of force guidelines, standard operating procedures, rules, and general orders.
- Investigate police misconduct.
- Investigate all police shootings, including all police involved shootings that kill unarmed people.
- Provide increased transparency of all investigations, including police involved shootings, and greater statistical analysis of demographic information of complaints by type and victim.
- Increase rates at which complaints are sustained based on thorough investigations of all allegations of police misconduct and violations of the US Constitution and Human Rights' law.
- Be the final authority regarding discipline in the Chicago Police Department.

- Indict police officers for crimes they commit.
- Establish its own budget.
- Replace the current rubber-stamp Chicago Police Board.
- Take over the job of the Independent Police Review Authority (IPRA) and eliminate it.
- Reduce bias and guarantee fair treatment of victims of police misconduct.
- Ensure police districts are racially and ethnically equitable and proportional to the communities they serve.
- Make simple complaint forms available to anyone, at city hall, all public libraries, and all police department district headquarters.
- Encourage UN Human Rights Commission to audit Chicago Police standards and their implementation.
- Establish a Police Pension Review Board.
- Assign a civilian to be Chief of the Internal Affairs Division, as in New Orleans.
- Increase community outreach and involvement in police districts.
- The power to petition the Chief Judge of the U.S. District Court to allow criminal charges before a sitting grand jury when police commit a crime such as battery, unlawful arrest, racial profiling, torture, rape, and murder when committed by police officers. (para. 4)

The *Anti Police-Terror Project* (2019a) has been a leading voice in community-based self-determinism. Using their grassroots power, they have levied the California Senate to pass legislation, *Assembly Bill 392: The California Act to Save Lives*, establishing one of the most restrictive police use of force standards in the country. The *Anti Police-Terror Project* (2019a) argued:

> Under current law, California police officers can use deadly force if it is "reasonable" regardless of whether deadly force was necessary to prevent imminent death or serious bodily injury, whether there were available alternatives, or whether the officer's own actions created the circumstances that led to the use of deadly force. AB 392 raises that standard to require that officers only use deadly force when "necessary to defend against an imminent threat of death or serious bodily injury to the officer or to another person." California would be the only state to combine this "necessary" standard with the requirement that courts consider an officer's conduct leading up to a use of deadly force when determining whether the officer's actions were justified. (para. 6)

This legislation could also have a significant future impact on the issue of qualified immunity for policing, opening the door for additional state actions that could add more stringent *necessity* standards, restricting the ability of police officers to use deadly force. Currently, the *qualified immunity doctrine* protects police officers "from liability for civil damages insofar as their conduct does not violate *clearly established* statutory or constitutional rights of which a reasonable person would have known" (Pearson v. Callahan, 555 U.S. 223, 231, 2009). Within this legal framework, the Supreme Court has interpreted "clearly established" under two separate components: A plaintiff must establish that it would have been clear to every reasonable police officer that the specific offending conduct was unconstitutional in the moment it was committed; and a plaintiff must establish clear legal precedent regarding the specific offending conduct. No precedent + no clearly established law = no police liability. According to the Crabbe, Brown & James LLP (2019, para. 3) General Counsel to the National Fraternal Order of Police (FOP) since 2001,

> Plaintiffs seeking to impose liability against law enforcement typically bring a § 1983 action for excessive force. A plaintiff can only overcome an officer's qualified immunity defense if they can show: (1) a significant injury; (2) that resulted from the use of clearly excessive force that violated the individual's Fourth Amendment rights; and (3) that the force used was objectively unreasonable, taking into account what a reasonable officer would do in the specific circumstances confronting the officer at the scene. (para. 3)

In addition, the *Anti Police-Terror Project* (2019b, para. 1–6) in an effort toward community self-determination and police abolition has set its sights on establishing a community-led *Independent Police Commission*. Within this framework, both a *Civilian Complaints Office* and a *Police Commission* would be established. This structure would act as a civilian system of checks and balances, with power centering on the will of the community. The Civilian Complaints Office would:

- Receive, investigate and resolve all civilian complaints against police in 120 days.
- Establish multiple in-person and online ways to submit, view and discuss complaints.
- Be immediately notified and required to send an investigator to the scene of a police shooting or in-custody death.
- Be allowed to interrogate officers less than 24 hours after an incident where deadly force is used.
- Access crime scenes, subpoena witnesses, and review files, with sanctions for non-compliance.
- Make disciplinary and policy recommendations to the Police Chief/Police Commission.

- Compel the Police Chief to explain why he/she has not followed a recommendation.
- Have the Police Commission decide cases where the Police Chief does not follow recommendations.
- Issue public quarterly reports analyzing complainants, demographics of complainants, status and findings of investigations and actions taken as a result of the recommendations.
- Be housed in a location separate from the police department.
- Be funded at an amount no less than 5% of the total police department budget.
- Have one investigator for every 70 police officers.
- Have its Director selected from candidates offered by community organizations.
- Not have current or former police officers or families of officers on its staff, including the Director. (para. 5)

The Police Commission would:

- Select its members from candidates proposed by community organizations.
- Determine policy for the Police Department based on community input and expertise.
- Share policy and proposed policy changes in publicly accessible formats.
- Discipline and dismiss police officers on referrals from the Civilian Complaints Office or the Police Chief.
- Hold public disciplinary hearings.
- Build a collectivist model of governance that assures highest levels of transparent accountability to the community.
- Select the candidates for the Police Chief to be hired by the Mayor or City Administrator.
- Evaluate and (if necessary) fire the Police Chief.
- Receive appropriate salaries based on effort required (suggested half time to start).
- Receive regular training on policing, principled community engagement and civil rights by community groups, impacted family members, and law enforcement personnel.
- Not have current, former or family of police officers as members. (para. 6)

Critical Resistance (2019b) was able to secure a significant policy-statement endorsement from the *American Public Health Association*, an influential 25,000 member D.C.-affiliated organization for public health professionals, providing support for an empirical argument that American policing is a public health issue. Using the American Public Health Association

(2018) report, *Addressing Law Enforcement Violence as a Public Health Issue, CR* (2019b) which details educational resources, recommended action steps, strategies, tactics, talking points, and facilitating notes, galvanizes the growing national narrative that policing is a public health issue.

However, legislation and policy statements enabling community control over policing and community justice-based initiatives are not enough. Abolishing policing requires power. Power to enforce the universal tenets of truth, justice, balance, harmony, order, righteousness, and reciprocity. Power to *learn to speak the language of police abolition.* Power to *unfriend policing.* Power to *decolonize the state narrative.* Power to mandate *community self-determinism.* Power that lead to the establishment of the community mindset and tools for the natural right of Black self-defense.

Chapter 5

Black Armed Resistance

"Did you pull that alarm nigger?" As soon as the officer repeated it and begin to open his car door, I started to slowly back away into the large crowd. If you attack me with words, I fight you back with words. If you attack me with hands, I fight you back with hands. I quickly blended into the crowd. I saw one of my classmates picking up a rock, so I picked up a rock. We both threw rocks in the direction of the officers and ducked into the corner store. That instigated a storm of rocks and bottles directed at the officers, who after being struck, retreated back into their vehicles and fled the area. The corner quickly cleared out as a large fire truck arrived. The officers never even looked for me and I didn't care if they did. The incident shaped how I would interpret the concept of armed resistance forever. As a child, I learned to operationalize the construct of "liberation" within the worldview of the Black Liberation Army.

In this final chapter, I will focus on one of the most controversial, yet one of the most healing rituals required for dismantling the institution of policing in America: *Black armed resistance.* Robert F. Williams (1962, pp. 4–5), in *Negroes with Guns*, argued that whenever the Black diaspora decided to take up arms in self-defense across American history, white people, who he described as "moral weaklings and cowards," always backed down in fear of losing the mythology of their own lives. Elijah Muhammad (1965, 217), in *Message to the Blackman in America*, believed that this universal right of Black armed self-defense extended to protecting oneself from the police. In addition, Kwame Ture (1970, para. 28) in his testimony to the U.S. Senate emphasized that Black armed resistance is the last component to Black liberation. My organic critical autoethnographic journey across America, asking the Black diaspora one central question "How do we get policing out of our lives," is synergized through this sacred right. The ritual of *Black armed*

71

resistance invokes the universal right of self-defense, which sits at the cosmological center of what Ashby (2005) described as the Kemetic spiritual inheritance of the Black diaspora: *truth, justice, balance, harmony, order, righteousness,* and *reciprocity.* Armed resistance is engrained within the cultural DNA of the Black diaspora in America.

A HISTORY OF BLACK ARMED RESISTANCE

The Black radical tradition has been working to dismantle policing ever since the Barbados Slave Code of 1661 was used to legitimize the first slave patrols that secured the construct of white supremacy in the Carolinas, in the late seventeenth century. American policing today are slave patrols. American policing is the armed wing of white supremacy. The Black radical tradition has always been at war with policing. Armed resistance is the story of the Black diaspora. Never lose sight of these universal truths. Slave patrols, America's original perpetrators of the homoerotic stop-and-frisk fetish: police carnal violence (Curry, 2017). The infatuation of white males holding, touching, and handling captive Black male bodies for consumer fantasization immediately discovered there was a price to pay for their savage anti-Black crimes. Kerry Walters (2015) in *American Slave Revolts and Conspiracies*, Herbert Aptheker (1983) in *American Negro Slave Revolts*, Richard Price (1996) in *Maroon Societies: Rebel Slave Communities in the Americas*, and Alvin Thompson (2006) in *Flight to Freedom: African Runaways And Maroons in the Americas* provided clear evidence that armed resistance to white supremacy shifted the entire narrative of Black liberation. Armed maroon communities would hunt down slave patrols and introduce them to one of the central themes embraced one hundred years later by the Black Liberation Army (1971) in *Message to the Black Movement: A Political Statement from the Black Underground:*

> America must learn that Black people are not the eternal suffers, the universal prisoners, the only ones who can feel pain. Revolutionary violence is, therefore, not a tactic of struggle, but a strategy . . . forcing all those responsible for oppression to realize that they too can bleed, they too can feel our pain. Only when this is realized, will any just and equal decisions be made, will we be conceded our right to self-determination. (pp. 14–15)

To place this narrative into a construct that most white liberals can digest, on October 14, 1964, Martin Luther King Jr. was awarded the Nobel Peace prize, making him the youngest winner of the prize in its history (King, 1968). In 1959, five years before winning the prize and four years before his "I Have a Dream" speech, MLK articulated the Black radical tradition's response to American white supremacy and its evil rhetoric of domination and hegemony, as synergized by Ani (1994). King's (1968) response echoed the voices of Black armed resistance:

> Violence exercised in self-defense, which all societies from the most primitive to the most cultured and civilized, accept as moral and legal. The principle of self-defense, even involving weapons and bloodshed, has never been con- demned, even by Gandhi, who sanctioned it for those unable to master pure nonviolence. When the Negro uses force in self-defense, he does not forfeit sup- port—he may even win it, by the courage and self-respect it reflects. (pp. 12–15)

Martin Luther King Jr., who was an avid gun owner, was explicit in his support for armed self-defense (Johnson, 2014). In fact, King even sought a permit to carry a concealed gun in his car (Cobb, 2015; Johnson, 2014; Umoja, 2014). What MLK clearly understood was the exact same thing that maroon communities, Black civil war veterans, the Deacons for Defense, the BPP, the BLA, and millions of the Black diaspora across America today that own guns clearly understand: the institution of white supremacy fears armed Black people (Williams, 1962). Always have, and always will. Frederick Douglass's advice of a good revolver, as the best response to slave catcher (Johnson, 2014), resonates with the Black diaspora today. So does W. E. B. DuBois's warning that a double-barrel shotgun would be used to spray the guts of a white mob (Umoja, 2014). As does Fannie Lou Hammer's words that she kept a shotgun at every corner of her bedroom and would not hesitate to use them on the first white person to do her harm (Cobb, 2015). Let's not forget Marcus Garvey's voice, in that all people have gained their freedom through organized force (Johnson, 2014). Finally, Malcolm X's vision of Black liberation was not against using violence in self-defense, because he believed that it's not violence but intelligence (Williams, 1962). You see, the Black diaspora within the Black radical tradition have always affirmed the power of armed resistance and the natural right of self-defense.

Black people with guns sit at the heart of white fear in America. It disturbs the white-centered imagination, whether that's at an academic conference, an abolitionist meeting, or inside of a police department. A few years ago when I began to share some of my initial research findings during presenta- tions at the Academy of Criminal Justice Sciences and the American Society of Criminology, both considered top conferences within the criminal justice discipline, I was advised by two white faculty peers, who are perceived by other white educators to be prominent scholars in the subfield of abolition- ism, to really stay away from any topic involving abolitionism and Black armed resistance. Before literally laughing at them, I asked if they would like to amplify their thoughts, and one of them nervously uttered, "What are Afrikan Americans going to do with guns, someone might get hurt." The other paused for a moment and said, "If guns are required, then it's not really abolitionism." It is to be understood that their views echoed the white liberal agenda I've heard for decades regarding the topic of guns and Black people in America. Well, the Black voices within the diaspora tell a different story. A significant portion of the Black diaspora I've ever spoken to in this critical autoethnographic journey suggest that without armed self-defense, police abolition would be impossible. That armed self-defense shifts the policing narrative of Blackness. That armed self-defense shifts the public narrative of Blackness. That armed self-defense shifts the political narrative of Blackness. That armed self-defense shifts the cultural narrative of Blackness. That armed self-defense shifts the power dynamics of Blackness. That the harmony of safety, the balance of security, and the reciprocity of self-preservation are the responsibilities of the collective Pan-Afrikan diaspora, not the state.

ARMED RESISTANCE AS SPIRITUAL INHERITANCE

The foundational core for the Black diaspora who support the ritual of armed resistance lies in the historical truth of an Afrikan-centered spirituality. As already noted, Black people created the concept of justice on this planet. This concept of justice is reflected in the principles of *ma'at*. There is no higher human behavioral code that has been found anywhere in history (Hilliard, Williams, & Damali, 1987). *Ma'at* is based on seven core universal virtues: *truth, justice, balance, harmony, order, righteousness*, and *reciprocity*. These virtues are protected by the universal science of self-defense, which consists of three interconnective metaphysical levels: spiritual, mental, and physical (Ashby, 2005, pp. 18–138).

According to Balogun Abeegunde (2015) in *Afrikan Martial Arts: Discovering the Warrior Within* and T. J. Obi Desch (2008) in *Fighting for Honor: The History of African Martial Art in the Atlantic World*, the Kemites or ancient Egyptians were the first people on the planet to apply the science of self-defense, or what is referred to as the Afrikan system of self-defense: *Montu*. The *Montu arts* is what is commonly known today as the martial arts. *Montu* or *Montu-Ra* is manifested in Afrikan spirituality as the Kemite symbolic god of war. A warrior that would attack the enemies of *ma'at*, that is, the truth of the cosmic order of the universe. Montu was often depicted as a man with the head of a falcon wearing a headdress of two long plumes, a solar disk and the double uraeus. According to Baba Ifa Karade (1994) in *The Handbook of Yoruba Religious Concepts*, Monique Joiner Siedlak (2016) in *Seven African Powers: The Orishas*, Jade Asikiwe (2018) in *Melanin: The Gift of The Cosmos*, and Kaba Hiawatha Kamene (2019) in *Spirituality Before Religions: Spirituality is Unseen Science*, within the Afrikan metaphysical journey of universal self-defense, *Ogun*, the god of war of the Yoruba people of West Africa, manifested. *Ogun* is the ruler over the elements of nature, specifically steel, by which weapons can be made. Within the Afrikan metaphysical, someone in the position of a police officer would be considered a child of *Ogun*. For the Pan-Afrikan diaspora, this alone disqualifies American policing from ever being able to sit at the throne of truth and justice.

Today, nearly 20 percent of the Black diaspora in America own firearms. That's nearly 8.5 million Black firearm owners in America. Another 30 percent live with someone who owns a firearm. Additionally, nearly 60 percent of the Black diaspora in America perceive guns as not only a positive thing but, in many cases, a necessity (National African American Gun Association, 2019, para.1 1; Saad, 2019). The Black diaspora in record numbers are now joining gun clubs, going to gun ranges, and are participating in competitive shooting events. There are Black-owned gun clubs that hold concealed weapon registration seminars, along with voting registration campaigns across the country. In fact, in the spirit of Asante Shakur, Black women are now one of the fastest growing demographic groups in America who are purchasing guns (National African American Gun Association, 2019, para. 9). According to Cobb (2016):

Armed self-defense (or, to use a term preferred by some, "armed resistance") as part of Black struggle began not in the 1960s with angry "militant" and "radical" young Afro-Americans, but in the earliest years of the United States as one of African people's responses to oppression. This tradition, which culminates with the civil rights struggles and achievements of the mid-1960s, cannot be understood independently or outside its broader historical context. In every decade of the nation's history, brave and determined Black men and women picked up guns to defend themselves and their communities. (p. 1)

Arguably, a tipping point has been reached in America between the Black diaspora and American policing. Pan-Afrikan people must be prepared to defend and impose the will of their *resistance consciousness* (Ture, 1967a). Ture (1967a, 1972, 1986, 1996b, 1998) reminds us that revolutionary struggle is not an appeal for morality but a struggle to only obtain power. Black armed self- defense is power. Black armed self-defense is a prerequisite for abolishing policing, because it will shift the entire power dynamic of America. Black armed self-defense will transform the who, what, where, when, why, and how power is operationalized and applied in America but the Black diaspora worldwide.

Black armed self-defense forces an uncomfortable reality for the future of America. This is the reason why America, as a settler colony, has dedicated the last 400 years trying to disarm Black people (Avent, 2019). Black disarmament legislation started as early as 1680 in Virginia, which was immediately followed by other states barring gun ownership to Black people, including the Fugitive Slave Acts, the Black Codes, Jim Crow, the war on drugs, mass incarceration, police militarization, and the creation of legislation prohibiting convicted felons from legally possessing guns (Cobb, 2015). The Sentencing Project (2017) estimates that nearly one-third of all Black men in America are prohibited from legally owning a firearm. That's 4 million Black adult men, which does not include the hundreds of thousands of Black women who cannot legally possess a firearm and invoke their natural right of self-defense in America (Black Demographics, 2018).

According to Christian Davenport (2014) in *How Social Movements Die: Repression and Demobilization of the Republic of New Africa*, the concept of armed self-defense in Black communities is not anything new in Black liberation efforts. Advanced by the Republic of New Africa (RNA) as early as 1969, it is gaining renewed interest today. The RNA has long urged the Black diaspora to take up arms, as a display of political power, cultural power, and Black resistance. As already noted, the RNA maintains that a significant number of the Black diaspora in America are already supportive of armed self-defense.

WHY DO GUNS MATTER

According to Peter Gelderloos (2018) in *How Nonviolence Protects the State*, policing weaponizes nonviolence and uses it to exploit the weaknesses of the oppressed masses, arguing that nonviolence is a tactic that ultimately results in failure because it is *ineffective, racist, statist, patriarchal, tactically and strategically inferior*, and *delusional*. Gelderloos (2018) adds that throughout the history of the United States, a blind radicalized adherence to the tactic of non-violence, or what is rationalized as pathological nonviolence (Churchill, 2007), has created a plethora of leaders, policies, and movements that simply co-opt white supremacy.

What we often forget within the realm of the Black radical tradition, within the realm of Black radical resistance, is that nonviolence and violence are only tactics, not stand-alone mantras for Black liberation. Tactics, that is, effective tactics, are only actions that produce desired reactions. Effective tactics flow from effective strategies or organized game plans, which flow from effective goals or purposes. You choose the most effective tactics, whether violent or nonviolent, that are strategically organized and planned, in order to produce your most desired result (Black Liberation Army, 1971; Muntaqim, 1997, 2010; Nkrumah, 1968; Sankara, 1988). Thus, this leaves us with several critical unanswered questions. If we acknowledge that white supremacy is violence and that policing is the antithesis of white supremacy violence, what are the most effective tactics or diversity of tactics, violence and/or nonviolence, to fight white supremacy and abolish policing? Is armed resistance or the threat of armed resistance a tactic of violence or nonviolence?

The historical inheritance of the Black diaspora in America is one of armed resistance. We have never critically understood or measured the long-term effect that an armed Black revolutionary mindset has played on the psyche of white America. Can we honestly attribute any success for Black liberation in America to nonviolence? Does anyone really believe that two centuries and hundreds of armed Black revolts (Balagoon, 2019; Clarke, 1992) and over 200,000-armed Black veterans of the Civil War (Johnson, 2014: Umoja, 2014) did not impact every single Black liberation effort, including those framed as reformist or nonviolent, over the last 155 years? Are we to believe that "sit-ins," "hunger strikes," and "petitions" ended the enslavement of 4 million Black people in America? Black people who have historically armed themselves with guns have left us with a formula for liberation. Nearly every so-called nonviolent Black political activist in American history, including MLK, carefully crafted a public narrative that used Black revolutionary armed violence as the rationale outcome, if their nonviolent reformist demands were not met. American policing prefers the Pan-Afrikan diaspora to be passive, nonviolent, and unarmed. Nonviolence in the hands of the police has been and continue to be a colonial enterprise. Nonviolence assures a police monopoly on armed violence, by creating a worldview where policing is the only legitimate source of armed self-defense. American policing recognizes that organized Black revolutionary activism poses a great threat to their power. The institution of policing has also read Fanon (1967) and understands the science of colonization and social control. Armed violence works. Armed violence is built into the culture of American policing, and thus armed violence is the only language that white supremacy respects or understands (Black Liberation Army, 1971; Muntaqim, 1997, Nkrumah, 1968; Sankara, 1988).

Is it fair to conclude that Black social movements today, which includes BLM, are reformist and nonviolent by nature, and because they are rewarded by white liberals and their media outlets who provide them with funding and choose their leadership to remain nonviolent, they will forever be powerless and be instruments of American policing. White liberalism is a product of the State. We must never forget this. White liberalism helps the police legitimize its violence against Black liberation through structural violence. Is the biggest impediment to police abolition today the Black social movements themselves? Gelderloos (2018) adds:

> If a movement is not a threat, it cannot change a system based on centralized coercion and violence and if that movement does not realize and exercise power that makes it a threat, it cannot destroy such a system. They [policing] cannot be persuaded by appeals to their conscience. We must reclaim histories of resistance, to understand why we have failed in the past and how exactly we achieved the limited success we did. Realizing that nonviolence has never actually produced historical victories towards revolutionary goals opens the door to considering other serious faults of nonviolence. (pp. 37–38)

According to Kuwasi Balagoon (2019) in *A Soldier's Story: Revolutionary Writings by a New African Anarchist*, being Black is a political condition that mandates liberation through scientific and organized armed resistance. Similar to many of the men I spoke with during the writing of my upcoming book, it was during his time of incarceration that he began to see clearly just how weak and fragile the nature of policing had become. As an incarcerated student, Balagoon formed political study groups that centered on Black liberation and decolonization efforts. Applying principles of CRT, given that white supremacy was a permanent component in American policing, it was the right of the Black diaspora to dismantle, expropriate, abolish, and liberate itself from policing through armed resistance. Balagoon (2019) argued:

> It is the right of the people to alter or abolish it. . . . The Slave Patrols were the predecessors of the fugitive squad, Red Squad, and Joint Terrorism Task Forces of today. Black communities must be prepared for an armed struggle and obtain concealed weapons permits. Others will be organized to infiltrate members into the U.S. Armed Forces, correctional departments, security firms, police departments, to obtain hard intelligence, and training as well as access to arms. For the police to stop the movement, they would have to arrest the entire community. (pp. 106–344)

POLICING THE POLICE

The question that morphed into almost every conversation on Black armed resistance was on the constitutionality of *policing the police*. That is, is there a Second Amendment right to arm yourself and to defend either yourself or others against police violence? The dearth of scholarly information on this topic was surprising, especially considering the history of the Black radical tradition and the growing level of frustration toward police violence directed at Black communities nationwide. According to Joshua Bloom and Waldo Martin (2016) in *Black against Empire: The History and Politics of the Black Panther Party*, the Panthers, the vanguards of scholar revolutionaries, described the use of firearms within constitutional terms, arguing that the Second Amendment provided them the legal right to carry firearms, in order to defend themselves and Black communities from police violence. In fact, this legal reasoning was put on full display as the Panthers routinely monitored police scanners and would randomly show up to police dispatched calls in Black neighborhoods, armed with loaded rifles and their criminal codebooks, monitoring and essentially *policing the police*. At the time, the State of California legally permitted the open display of firearms in public locations. However, this display of Black power prompted California to immediately draft legislation, repealing the right for anyone to openly carry firearms in public, effectively ending the Panthers creation of Black community policing (Newton, 1972), still leaving unanswered questions regarding the constitutionality of deadly force in self-defense against police violence.

Within the Pan-Afrikan diaspora today, the *Huey P. Newton Gun Club* (2019) has again placed the platform of using armed resistance in policing the police, at the forefront. Based out of Dallas, Texas, the Huey P. Newton Gun Club (2019) describes itself as:

> A coalition of members from various different groups/organizations coming together in unity to practice our 2nd amendment right "To bear Arms." Our mission is to educate the masses of people on the necessity of self. That includes self-preservation, self-defense, and self-sufficiency through militant culture. Safety, caution, and attention to detail are at the core of our way of life. We desire a world of peace, justice, and equality for all humanity, and specifically people of color. (para. 1)

Originally formed around 2010, the Huey P. Newton Gun Club's primary focus centered on issues of police brutality, given the Dallas Police Department's long history and track record of racial violence and bloodshed against the Black community. Establishing armed community patrols to counter police violence, the Huey P. Newton Gun Club (2019) articulated one key local objective—*To Develop and Enforce Accountability in Law Enforcement and the Criminal Justice System*:

> We respect the Police in our community who show proper respect for our community. We respect those in authority as long as they respect us. We, the Huey P Newton Gun Club, mobilize and organize for an end to police brutality and misconduct. We demand the police in our community, and elsewhere, respect the Human Rights of our people and their constitutional rights. We strive for

community police review boards with legal power to seek indictments, punish and discipline rogue police officers. We will monitor and observe the police according to the law. We struggle to reform areas in our community or nation from the negative behavior that is imposed upon us. We believe in our divine and legal rights to self-defense after centuries of state regulated abuse and terrorism. The criminal justice system must be held accountable to the will of our people, and not support an industrial complex, capitalizing in profit to see our people continuously incarcerated. (para. 3)

Largely embraced for their strong educational platform regarding armed self-defense and their advocacy for arming every single Black person in America, almost ten years into their existence, the Huey P. Newton Gun Club has inspired a new era of Black armed nationalism. Interest not only in gun ownership but in how armed resistance can be utilized to empower Black communities over police violence has never been higher.

According to Darrell Miller (2011, pp. 939–976), a professor of law at Duke University School of Law, in *Retail Rebellion and the Second Amendment*, and Kindaka Sanders (2015, pp. 695–750), a professor of law at the Thurgood Marshall School of Law at Texas Southern University, in *A Reason to Resist: The Use of Deadly Force in Aiding Victims of Unlawful Police Aggression*, a compelling argument can be made for armed resistance against police violence. Miller (2011, p. 939) and Sanders (2015, p. 701) argue that in *District of Columbia v. Heller*, the Supreme Court held that self-defense lies at the core of the Second Amendment and that it codifies a natural right, for both individuals and communities, to keep and bear arms for self-defense, which extends to both private and public threats, including self-defense against government violence. Miller (2011) and Sanders (2015) argue in *McDonald v. City of Chicago* that the Supreme Court in deeming the Second Amendment a fundamental right highlighted its role in protecting newly freed Black people, enabling them to bear arms for defense against rogue law enforcement officers seeking to disarm them. According to the *Official Report of the Supreme Court* (2010) Justice Clarence Thomas wrote about the aftermath of Nat Turner's 1831 slave rebellion in Virginia, declaring:

> The fear generated by these and other rebellions led Southern legislatures to take particularly vicious aim at the rights of free blacks and slaves to speak or to keep and bear arms for their defense. (p. 585)

The Court added that the right to keep and bear arms for self-defense includes the ability to defend yourself against tyrannical local or state violence. Miller (2011) explained:

Among the McDonald Court's reasons was a recognition that, during Reconstruction, local law enforcement was, in fact, behaving tyrannically. Local police and recusant state militias terrorized freedmen, sometimes alone, sometimes in collusion with unofficial citizen patrols and groups like the Klan. If one of the principal aims of the Civil Rights Act of 1866 and the Fourteenth Amendment was to allow freedmen to arm themselves in order to repel unreconstructed Southern law enforcement, then it seems that modern individuals would enjoy a constitutional right to publicly arm themselves in case they need to threaten, to resist, or even to fire upon police officers who violate the law. (p. 943)

While the Supreme Court's interpretation of the Second Amendment establishes that there is a right to use armed resistance against the police, the Court failed to provide any specific guidance, scope, or limitations regarding the contours of such a right, as well as whether this right would extend to third-party defense (Miller, 2011; Sanders, 2015). Because the legal interpretation is so ambiguous, the overwhelming majority of the states, with strong support from FOP unions, have criminalized even resisting the police for an unlawful arrest. Today, less than thirteen states allow a person to resist an unlawful. However, Miller (2011, pp. 974–976) argues that the Constitution does provide a refuge—the jury. That is, any claim and evidence of armed self-defense in reaction to unlawful police violence must be presented to a jury, where natural law meets positive law. "The natural right to self-preservation can never be sequestered from the jury" (p. 976).

According to Sanders (2015, p. 696), due to this legal ambiguity, the Indiana Supreme Court abolished the English common law right to resist an unlawful arrest, under *Barnes v. State.* Sanders (2015) noted:

The U.S. Supreme Court has not directly considered the question of whether citizens can use deadly force in defending against unlawful police force. However, in John Bad Elk [John Bad Elk v. United States], the Court implied that the defendant could have used deadly force against police officers who were about to use deadly force against him. At common law, a citizen had the right to use deadly force against a police official using unnecessary, deadly force in effecting a lawful arrest. Most states have not abridged this common law rule. (p. 728)

In 2012, in reaction to what many Indianans perceived as a major infringement on gun owners' rights of self-defense, the Indiana State Legislature enacted an unprecedented first-of-its-kind statute, *Indiana Code § 35–41–3–2,* authorizing the use of force, with an extension for third-party defense, to include the use of deadly force against public servants acting unlawfully against the persons or property of Indiana citizens. Within this narrative,

Sanders (2015, pp. 696) argues a compelling issue, specifically as it relates to Black armed resistance: the Supreme Court has opened Pandora's box on legislation similar to *Indiana Code § 35–41–3-2* to be enacted across the nation, where the use or threatened use of defensive force against unlawful police violence may in fact serve as a real deterrent for police misconduct involving excessive force in Black communities.

In doing so, Sanders (2015, p. 740) makes an argument that Black communities across America, as the most targeted population for racialized unlawful police violence in the history of this country, going back to policing's origins as slave patrols and rising through the ranks of the Black Codes, Jim Crow, and COINTELPRO, are the most in need of Second Amendment and subsequent specific state legislative statutes, to establish the legal right of armed self-defense, including third-party armed self-defense, against tyrannical police misconduct and associated police violence. Additionally, Sanders (2015, p. 744) argues that armed Black community patrols who have a widespread understanding of armed self-defense, like those discussed in this chapter and whose actions are already upheld by the Second Amendment, could be invaluable in curbing unlawful police violence. Sanders (2015) notes:

> The Second Amendment as recently interpreted in *McDonald* and *Heller* provides the vehicle for the effective use of [armed] community patrols and intervention. State statutes that describe the right to defend in resistance will provide further clarity and thus will help empower citizens to challenge individualized government tyranny in their communities. (p. 745)

Just imagine if similar legislation were passed in every state across the nation. This initiative would have a deep and broad ripple effect on the real-world power relationship between policing and the Pan-Afrikan diaspora. Black armed resistance, supported with groundbreaking state legislation similar to *Indiana Code § 35–41–3-2*, with a clear understanding of their constitutional rights of self-defense against unlawful police violence, could play a significant role in the systemic abolishment of policing in America, which leaves us with one final lingering question. We already have tens of thousands of armed and trained Black police officers in America. What role, if any, should these Black police officers play in armed resistance?

THE ROLE OF BLACK POLICE OFFICERS IN ARMED RESISTANCE

Do Black police officers have a role in dismantling systems of white supremacy? Do Black police officers have a role in abolishing policing? Do Black police officers have a role in armed resistance? Clearly, some of the most critically challenging series of questions I faced writing this book. Better yet, maybe the questions should be, "Do Black police officers *want to play a role* in dismantling systems of white supremacy, abolishing policing, and armed resistance?"

According to the U.S. Department of Justice (2015) in *Local Police Departments, 2013: Personnel, Policies, and Practices*, and the Pew Research Center (2019) in *Behind the Badge: Inside America's Police Departments*, there is a dearth of data on Black police officers in America. Although there are no gender-specific data, it is estimated that Black officers make up between 11 and 12 percent of the total 750,000–800,000 police officers in America. Thus, estimates indicate there are roughly between 83,000 and 96,000 Black police officers in America. There is no data on the exact number of Black police chiefs that lead America's 18,000+ police agencies, but if the number of prison wardens or district attorneys is any indication, we're not looking at more than 3–4 percent.

During my thirty-eight-year critical autoethnographic and metaphysical odyssey examining the policing culture in America, conversing with over a thousand Black police officers around the country, my findings continue to evolve on whether Black officers actually *want to play a role* in Black liberation. However, let me discuss one consistent theme: the overwhelming majority of Black police officers in America do not represent the ideological platform of the conscious Pan-Afrikan diaspora. This is a very important fact that should be understood. Black police recruits are carefully screened, to ensure their serviceability to a white policing culture. Thus, the policing culture attracts and retains, by the very nature of its historic purpose, colonized Black minds. Liberated Black minds need not apply. Black recruits are vetted through a system of white supremacy that ensures this level of quality control. Ture (1967a) would refer to this type of Black police officer as an *assimilado*. It is nearly impossible to make it through the hiring process if you acknowledge or if it is discovered that your loyalty is to the advancement of the Pan-Afrikan experience, rather than to the institution of policing and everything that entails. It is to be kept in mind that these Black police recruits understand that racism can exist in policing but rationalize it to the "bad apple" narrative pushed by the policing culture. The Black policing culture lives in a state of cognitive dissonance.

Secondly, the policing culture purchases the loyalty and silence of their Black police contingent, by feeding them three seductive poisons: greed, anger, and ignorance. According to *Police Officers* (2018), the median salary for a police officer is over $67,000, which is about $15,000 more than the average national salary of $52,000 and about $25,000 more than the median household income for a Black family at $41,511 (Brookings Institution,

2019). As a Black male and former police officer myself, and having spoken to countless Black police officers nationwide, I have rarely met an officer who was not making at least $100,000 annually. In addition, Black police officers are fed by the culture, the temporary illusion of power, and the temporary illusion of privilege, separating them from the Black masses in America, as long as they are willing to enforce and protect the mandates of the state. Black police officers become addicted to the financial rewards and the illusion of temporary entitlements lived daily by their white peers.

The policing culture then assigns the overwhelming majority of Black police officers to work in Black communities, to *police their own*, in order to reinforce the colonization process and to appeal to their innate anger. You see, fueled by a system of white supremacy, many of these Black police officers have an innate anger, resentment, and fear toward certain Black people, specifically Black males, who do not fit into their own comfortable narrative of Black respectability and white American assimilation. Justifiably, the cultural and political blow-back that Black police officers receive from Black communities, again, specifically Black males, is indescribable. I would argue because of this, many Black police officers spend their entire careers trying to *socially apologize* to Black communities. These officers feel embarrassed, shamed, humiliated, and trapped by their daily interactions with a Black community that does not fear, respect, or tolerate their very presence. Using the tactics of their institutional colonizers, Black police officers lash out with direct and structural brutality against the very same Black faces they see daily in the community, in their own families, and in their own mirrors. There is a reason why a dearth of research exists on alcohol/substance abuse, domestic violence, divorce rates, impact on children, and so forth specifically for Black police officers in America. The self-inflicted psychic violence absorbed by Black police officers keeps them cycling in and out of a wicked state of double consciousness. Franz Fanon (1952) in the epic *Black Skin, White Masks* discusses this powerful level of cognitive dissonance within the hyper-colonized psyche. However, Black police officers understand that stopping, frisking, arresting, and brutalizing Black bodies are also directly tied to their salaries via overtime, provide them with the opportunity to apply their temporary power and privilege, and reinforce their value to fellow white police officers and the policing institution. Black police officers see Black male bodies as social and economic capital. The poisons of greed and anger blend into one.

A culture of ignorance also appeals to Black police officers, whether willful or unintentional. Within this climate, a Black police officer does not care about anyone but their own individual survival. The Black community becomes invisible. Their anger has been replaced by obliviousness. They don't want to see, hear, or talk about police misconduct in Black neighborhoods. They don't want to stop, frisk, or arrest any Black bodies. They don't want the overtime money. They don't want the temporary illusion of power or privilege that comes with being a Black police officer. They want to come to work, put on their blinders, get a dinner break, put their blinders back on, and go back home. They don't want any racial drama. They are fully aware of the fact that they are working in a system of white supremacy. They do not want to be a witness against the white policing culture. They have witnessed the predatory contempt the policing culture has displayed against Black police officers that have spoken out against institutional white supremacy within policing, and they want no part of it. Policing is all they have. Without policing, they become part of the so-called Black underclass in America they police every day. So, all they do is duck and hide for twenty-five years until retirement.

Based on my research findings, I have just described the overwhelming majority of Black police officers in America. Fueled by the poisons of greed, anger, and/or ignorance, many actively work to maintain the system of white supremacy we know as American policing. But what about the others? Well, what I've discovered is that there is a small portion of Black police officers that aggressively work to expose individual acts of racism within the policing culture, both internally and externally, and work very hard to hold those officers accountable for their racist behavior. These officers have created their own Black police unions, Black police organizations, Black police social media platforms, and Black community policing outreach projects. Because they are so outspoken on issues of racism, many are harassed and ridiculed by their fellow officers. The problem is, these same Black police officers who fight to expose police misconduct and demand police accountability in Black communities still trust, believe in, and are loyal to the institution of American policing. That is, they acknowledge that racism can be systemic, but refuse to acknowledge that policing is a system of white supremacy. They believe that the overwhelming majority of police officers are not racist but are dedicated to the tenets of justice, service, and peace. They acknowledge that body cameras and implicit bias training have little or no impact on curbing race-based police misconduct but believe recruiting/hiring more Black police officers, developing better community policing strategies in Black communities, and promoting more Black police chiefs are viable solutions. They believe in procedural justice, place-based policing, focused deterrence, and predictive policing. They believe in the growth of American policing. They believe in the institution of American policing.

However, in my research I have also discovered a very small but growing outlier of Black police officers who are conscious of the collective nature of the Black diaspora and have centered their own Blackness as a priority above the systemic identity of the policing culture. Black police officers who acknowledge that racism is a systemic problem in policing and that white supremacy fuels the institution of policing. In fact, these officers believe it's their moral duty to confront and fight white supremacy within the institution on a daily basis. This comes not only in the form of police accountability but in the realization that policing as an institution cannot be trusted to do the right thing for the Black experience in America, at any time. They are committed to speaking out on the record, against all forms of police misconduct. They are committed to speaking truth to power, including discrediting police unions. They are committed to removing policing, all forms of policing, from Black communities. They support drastically reducing the number of police officers recruited/hired, slashing budgets, and eliminating overtime funding. They understand that policing is the problem.

So, where do Black police officers fall on the continuum of abolishing American policing? The overwhelming majority would never willingly support it, for the plethora of reasons, I've already discussed. But that's right now. The policing culture is not getting any better. High rates of substance abuse, divorce, suicide, and domestic violence place the policing culture as one of the most self-destructive and toxic environments in the nation (Addictions Center, 2019; Hilliard, 2019; National Center for Women & Policing, 2019). In addition, the policing culture is not getting any Blacker. Black police officer employment rates nationwide have basically stalled, with only a 3 percent increase over the past thirty-five years. In fact, there has been virtually no change in Black police employment rates over the last seven years (U.S. Department of Justice, 2015). Policing, by its very nature of cultural exploitation and colonization, is slowly beginning to shift away from focusing on Black officer candidates while increasing its efforts at securing the services of more Latinx police officers, which is creating its own unique set of policing cultural dynamics. The money in immigration violence is just too much to pass on. In the very near future, as Black police officer demographics begin to fall and as their cultural capital within the institution of policing diminishes, perhaps an evolution of Black consciousness will take place. It would not surprise me given the nature of the universe and how Karma or *Ari* plays itself out. Black police officers have a keen awareness of the fragile nature of the policing culture and could collectively damage the institution's immune system and play their own unique role in applying the five interwoven rituals for police abolition.

FINAL THOUGHTS

Today, the institution of policing, the armed wing of white supremacy in America, finds itself fragile, impotent, and ripe for being dismantled. The police murders of George Floyd, Breonna Taylor, Ahmaud Arbery, and Rashard Brooks, all within a few weeks of each other, have triggered a *wave of delegitimization*. A growing segment of white liberals no longer trust, respect, or more importantly, fear dismantling American policing. This is crucial when you understand that the only demographic responsible for maintaining the institution of American policing today are white liberals. However, what most people fail to understand is that policing in America runs off an algorithm, based on white passive acceptance. That is, policing in America, numbering at less than one million full and part-time police officers, has no real power unless several hundred million white people passively accept and recognize their authority. Any level of active resistance by the white masses overwhelms the ability of policing to maintain any level of control or authority; hence the use of the National Guard and/or US Military as support mechanisms was brought in to save policing during uprisings and demonstrations in 2020. When that level of resistance becomes organized and hits critical mass, let's say 5 percent of the white adult population, policing will be dismantled. However, as noted throughout this book, white liberals in America and the institution of policing share mutual interests; hence, this scenario is extremely improbable, unlikely, and completely hopeless.

Kwame Nkrumah (1968), in *Handbook of Revolutionary Warfare*, argued that only through the collective revolutionary lens of the Pan-Afrikan masses, can we abolish worldwide systems of oppression. That we must all embrace the struggle of revolutionary resistance. That we must know who we are resisting, what we are resisting, when we are resisting, where we are resisting, why we are resisting, and how we are resisting. I hope this book serves as a starting point for a collective truth, in understanding that the Black diaspora's resistance of American policing is in fact a global resistance to all state oppression. That everyone benefits from the truth cemented in the fearless radical Black tradition. The words of Salathiel Thompson, a formerly incarcerated professor who co-taught a groundbreaking University of Pittsburgh course at Federal Bureau of Prisons (BOP) FCI McKean in 2016, *ADMJ 1449: Special Topics-The United States of America vs. The United States of America* (Gaskew, 2016), best illustrates this truth:

> In the beginning was the Aboriginal Afrakan. The Aboriginal Afrakan populated the earth and became other races. All other races must return too and in acknowledgement of themselves as children of the Afrakan parent-stock. It is my duty to introduce an Afrakan consciousness, a bridge between the individual micro and the societal macro, the only universal language of truth. I witnessed firsthand, the liberating power of the truth of the information I imparted, which did not place one over the other, nor at the expense of the other, but rather served to round out and elucidate the existing information, placing it in its proper

historical perspective, place, and time, and thus enhancing it. This is our first
universal truth. (as cited in Gaskew & Thompson, 2020b, pp. 19–23)

Remember, policing is just a hustle. A greed injected American hustle. A
hustle that depends on the mass exploitation and extinction of Black bodies
as capitol. It's only a matter of time before 40 million plus Black people in
America decide they no longer want to be hustled, and then *Black against
empire*. There can be no conditions in our fight for Black liberation except
those set by the Black diaspora. Anyone who claims that American policing
does not recognize the real danger in allowing the Black diaspora to organize
its full blown physical, intellectual, and spiritual capacity to wage revolution
for dismantling the institution of policing is living in denial of the universal
law of *truth, justice, balance, harmony, order, righteousness*, and *reciprocity*.
During this critical autoethnographic journey, I heard the voices of the
Black radical tradition in America, and they are organizing for a life without
policing. Organizing their Black consciousness. Organizing their Black resistance. Organizing their Black fearlessness. Organizing their ancestral minds,
bodies, and spirits for the ritual of revolution by *speaking the language of
police abolition, unfriending policing, decolonizing the state narrative, man-
dating community self-determination,* and *embracing Black armed resistance*.
These are the lessons I've learned from the front lines of Black liberation.

References

Abagond, J. (2016.) *Micah Xavier Johnson – a rant in 500 words or less*. Retrieved from https://abagond.wordpress.com/2016/07/09/micah-xavier-johnson-a-rant-in -500-words-or-less/

Abdulmumit, J. (2018). *Black Radical Movement Needs Infrastructure*. The Black Agenda Report. Retrieved from https://www.blackagendareport.com/jihad-abdul mumit-black-radical-movement-needs-infrastructure

Abeegunde, B. (2008). *Afrikan Martial Arts: Discovering the Warrior Within*. Atlanta, GA: Boss Up Inc.

Abu-Jamal, M. (2003). *Faith of Our Fathers: An Examination of the Spiritual Life of Africa*, Trenton, NJ: Africa World Press.

Abu-Jamal, M. (2016). *We Want Freedom*: *A Life in the Black Panther Party*. Brooklyn, NY: Common Notions Publications.

Adams, M., & Rameua, M. (2016). *Black Community Control Over Police*. Wisconsin Law Review. Retrieved from http://wisconsinlawreview.org/wp-content/uploads/2 016/06/4-Adams-Rameau-Final.pdf

Addictions Center. (2019). *The Relationship Between Addiction and Emergency Responders*. Retrieved from https://www.addictioncenter.com/addiction/emergenc y-responders/

African Poems-Oral Poetry from Africa. (2019). *Ogun, God of War*. Retrieved from https://africanpoems.net/gods-ancestors/ogun-god-of-war/

Afrika, L. (2009). *Melanin: What Makes Black People Black*. New York, NY: Seaburn Publishing.

Akbar, N. (1994). *Light from Ancient Africa*. Tallahassee, FL: Mind Production & Associates, Inc.

Al-Amin. J.A. (1969). *Die Nigger Die: A Political Autobiography*. Chicago, IL: Lawrence Hill Books.

Allen, J. (2014) *After Nevada Ranch Stand-Off, Emboldened Militias Ask: Where Next?* Retrieved from https://www.reuters.com/article/us-usa-ranchers-ne

vada-militia-insight/after-nevada-ranch-stand-off-emboldened-militias-ask-where-next-idUSBREA3G26620140417

American Public Health Association. (2018). *Addressing Law Enforcement Violence as a Public Health Issue*. Retrieved from https://www.apha.org/policies-and-advocacy/public-health-policy-statements/policy-database/2019/01/29/law-enforcement-violence

Anderson, J. (2012). A Tension in the Political Thought of Huey P. Newton. *Journal of African American Studies*, *16*(2), 249–267.

Ani, M. (1994). *Yurugu: An African-Centered Critique of European Cultural Thought and Behavior*. Trenton, NJ: Africa World Press.

Anti Police-Terror Project. (2019a). *Anti Police-Terror Project Statement on AB 392, the California Act to Save Lives*. Retrieved from http://www.antipoliceterrorproject.org/california-act-to-save-lives-ab-392

Anti Police-Terror Project. (2019b). *Oakland Should Lead the Way: Proposal for Effective Police Oversight*. Retrieved from http://www.antipoliceterrorproject.org/oakland-should-lead-the-way-proposal-for-effective-police-oversight

Aptheker, H. (1983). *American Negro Slave Revolts*. New York, NY: International Publishing Company.

Ashby, M. (2005). *Introduction to MA'AT Philosophy*. Lithonia, GA: The Sema Institute.

Ashby, M. (2008). *The Kemetic Tree of Life Ancient Egyptian Metaphysics and Cosmology for Higher Consciousness*. Lithonia, GA: The Sema Institute.

Asikiwe. J. (2018). *Melanin: The Gift of the Cosmos*. Scotts Valley, CA: CreateSpace Independent Publishing Platform.

Avent, Q. (2019). *African Americans and the 2nd Amendment: The Need for Black Armed Self-Defense*. The Carolinian. Retrieved from https://carolinianuncg.com/2019/02/20/african-americans-and-the-2nd-amendment-the-need-for-black-armed-self-defense/

A World Without Police. (2019). *Imagine a World Without Police*. Retrieved from http://aworldwithoutpolice.org/

Balagoon, K. (2019). *A Soldier's Story: Revolutionary Writings by a New African Anarchist*. Montreal, QC: Kersplebedeb Publishing.

Baldwin, J. (1961). *The Negro in American Culture*. *CrossCurrents, 11*(3), 205–224.

Baldwin, J. (1966). *A Report from Occupied Territory*. The Nation.

Ball, P. (2019). *Violence in Blue: Police Homicides in the United States*. Granta. Retrieved from https://granta.com/violence-in-blue/

Baltimore Bloc. (2019). *#WANTEDWEDNESDAY*. Retrieved from http://baltimorebloc.com/?fbclid=IwAR2KibvtELbo1D1nwjA2AbDLUMuWOkXHrniWbnr68L6vKhr1c8gT4JwhcIw

Bell, D. (1984). *A Holiday for Dr. King: The Significance of Symbols in the Black Freedom Struggle*, 17 U.C. Davis L. Rev. 433.

Bell, D. (1987). *And We Are Not Saved: The Elusive Quest for Racial Justice*. New York, NY: Basic Books.

Bell, D. (1988). *White Superiority in America: Its Legal Legacy, Its Economic Costs*, 33 Vill. L. Rev. 767.

Bell, D. (1990). *Racial Reflections: Dialogues in the Direction of Liberation*, 37 UCLA L. Rev. 1037.

Bell, D. (1992a). *Faces at the Bottom of the Well*. New York, NY: Basic Books.

Bell, D. (1992b). *Racial Realism*, 24 Conn. L. Rev. 363.

Bennett, L. (1961). *Before the Mayflower: A history of Black America*. New York, NY: Penguin Books.

Bennet, R. (2011). *The Black and Tans*. London: Pen and Sword Military.

Biondi, M. (2014). *The Black Revolution on Campus*. Los Angeles, CA: University of California Press.

Black Community Control of Police. (2017). *Black Community Control of Police Working Group*. [Video File]. Retrieved from https://www.facebook.com/Black -Community-Control-of-Police-559879807448690/

Black Demographics. (2018). *Black Male Statistics: Population*. Retrieved from http: //blackdemographics.com/population/black-male-statistics/

Black is Back Coalition (BIBC) of Social Justice, Peace, and Reparations. (2019). *Principles of Unity*. Retrieved from http://blackisbackcoalition.org/what-we-do/pr inciples-of-unity/

Black Liberation Army. (1971). *Message to the Black Movement: A Political Statement from the Black Underground*. Chico, CA: Abraham Guillen Press/Arm the Spirit.

Black Panther Party of Self Defense. (1970). *Police Petition*. Los Angeles, CA: Berkley Monitor Newsletter.

Blackstock, N. (1988). *COINTELPRO: The FBI's Secret War on Political Freedom*. Atlanta, GA: Pathfinder Press.

Bloom, J., & Martin, W. (2016*). Black against Empire: The History and Politics of the Black Panther Party*. Los Angeles, CA: University of California Press.

Bodhi, B. (2016). *The Buddha's Teachings on Social and Communal Harmony: An Anthology of Discourses from the Pali Canon*. Boston, MA: Wisdom Publications.

Boggs, J., & Boggs, G. L. (1974). *Revolution and Evolution in the Twentieth Century*. New York, NY: Monthly Review Press.

Bonilla-Silva, E. (2005). Racism and New Racism: The Contours of Racial Dynamics in Contemporary America. In Z. Leonardo (ed.), *Critical Pedagogy and Race*. Hoboken, NJ: Blackwell Publishing.

Bouche, T., & Rivard, L. (2013). *America's Hidden History: The Eugenics Movement*. Retrieved from https://www.nature.com/scitable/forums/genetics-ge neration/america-s-hidden-history-the-eugenics-movement-123919444/

Brookings Institution. (2019). *Black Household Income*. Retrieved from https://ww w.brookings.edu/blog/the-avenue/2019/10/03/black-household-income-is-rising -across-the-united-states/

Brown, V. (2010). *The Reaper's Garden: Death and Power in the World of Atlantic Slavery*. Cambridge, MA: Harvard University Press.

Brown, V. (2020). *Tacky's Revolt: The Story of an Atlantic Slave War*. Cambridge, MA: Belknap Press.

Bunseki, K. K. (2001). *African Cosmology of the Bantu-Kongo: Tying the Spiritual Knot, Principles of Life & Living*. Brooklyn, NY: UK: Athelia Henrietta Press.

Bureau of Justice Statistics. (2003). *Prevalence of Imprisonment in the U.S. Population, 197001*. Retrieved from http://www.bjs.gov/content/pub/pdf/piusp01.pdf

Bureau of Justice Statistics. (2017). *Race and Hispanic Origin of Victims and Offenders, 2015*. Retrieved from https://www.bjs.gov/content/pub/pdf/rhovo1215.pdf

Bureau of Justice Statistics. (2019). *Data Collection: National Crime Victimization Survey* (NCVS). Retrieved from https://www.bjs.gov/index.cfm?ty=dcdetail&iid=245

Carroll, C. (1900). *The Negro a Beast or In the Image of God*. Philadelphia, PA: American Book and Bible House.

Carson, C. (1981). *In Struggle: SNCC and the Black Awakening of the 1960s*. Cambridge, MA: Harvard UP.

Chicago Alliance Against Racial Repression. (2018). *Civilian Police Accountability Council*. Retrieved from http://naarpr.org/civilian-police-accountability-council-cpac/

Childress, S. (2017). *The Battle Over Bunkerville: The Bundys, the Federal Government and the New Militia Movement*. Frontline. Retrieved from https://www.pbs.org/wgbh/frontline/article/the-battle-over-bunkerville/

Churchill, W. (2007). *Pacifism as Pathology: Reflections on the Role of Armed Struggle in North America*. Chico, CA: AK Press.

Churchill, W., & Wall, J. (1990). *Agents of Repression: The FBI's Secret Wars Against the Black Panther Party and the American Indian Movement*. Boston, MA: South End Press.

Clarke, J. H. (1992). *Christopher Columbus and the African Holocaust: Slavery and the Rise of European Capitalism*. New York, NY: A & B Books.

Cleaver, E. (1968). *Soul on Ice*. New York: Dell Publications.

Cobb, C. (2015). *This Nonviolent Stuff'll Get You Killed: How Guns Made the Civil Rights Movement Possible*. Durham, NC: Duke University Press.

Collins, S. (2015). *'We Will Shoot Back': Meet the Black Activists Who Aren't Ready To Forgive*. ThinkProgress. Retrieved from https://thinkprogress.org/we-will-shoot-back-meet-the-black-activists-who-aren-t-ready-to-forgive-d53101387c31/

Crabbe, Brown, & James LLP (2019). *Critics of the Qualified Immunity Doctrine Seeking to Narrow Its Scope May Leave Law Enforcement Stuck Between A Rock and A Hard Place*. Retrieved from https://cbjlawyers.com/critics-of-the-qualified-immunity-doctrine-seeking-to-narrow-its-scope-may-leave-law-enforcement-stuck-between-a-rock-and-a-hard-place/

Crenshaw, K., Gotanda, N., Peller, G., &Thomas, K. (1995). *Critical Race Theory: The Key Writings that Formed the Movement*. New York, NY: The New Press.

Crichlow, V. (2017). The Solitary Criminologist. Constructing a Narrative of Black Identity and Alienation in the Academy. *Race and Justice*, 7(2), 179–195.

Critical Resistance. (2019a). *Abolishing Policing*. Retrieved from http://criticalresistance.org/abolish-policing/

Critical Resistance. (2019b). *Public Health is a Strategy for Abolition*. Retrieved from http://criticalresistance.org/wp-content/uploads/2019/05/APHA_pamphlet_FINAL_Feb201.pdf

Crow, S. (2018). *Setting Sights: Histories and Reflections on Community Armed Self-Defense.* Oakland, CA: PM Press.

Curry, T. (2017). *The Man-Not: Race, Class, Genre, and the Dilemmas of Black Manhood.* Philadelphia, PA: Temple University Press.

Davenport, C. (2014). *How Social Movements Die: Repression and Demobilization of the Republic of New Africa.* Boston, MA: Cambridge University Press.

Davis, A. (2005). *Abolition Democracy.* New York: Seven Stories Press.

Davis, J. (1992). *Spying on America: The FBI's Domestic Counter-Intelligence Program.* Santa Barbara, CA: Praeger.

Degruy, J. (2017). *Post Traumatic Slave Syndrome: America's Legacy of Enduring Injury and Healing.* Portland, OR: Joy Degruy Publications Inc.

Delgado, R., & Stefancic, J. (1993). Critical Race Theory: An Annotated Bibliography. *Virginia Law Review, 79*(2), 461–516.

Delgado, R., & Stefancic, J. (2017). *Critical Race Theory: An Introduction.* New York, NY: New York University Press.

Desch Obi, T. J. (2008). *Fighting for Honor: The History of African Martial Art in the Atlantic World.* Columbia, SC: University of South Carolina Press.

Divine, T. F. (2019). The Black One: Microaggressions in a Criminal Justice Program. In U. Thomas (ed.), *Navigating Micro-Aggressions Toward Women in Higher Education* (pp. 167–180). Hershey, PA: IGI Global.

Douglas, F. (1857). *West India Emancipation.* [Speech]. Delivered at Canandaigua, in New York.

DuBois, W. E. B. (1899). *The Philadelphia Negro.* Philadelphia, PA: University of Pennsylvania Press.

Edwards, F., Lee, H., & Esposito, M. (2019). *Risk of Being Killed by Police Use of Force in the United States by Age, Race–Ethnicity, and Sex.* Washington, DC: Proceedings of the National Academy of Sciences.

Ethical Society of Police. (2019). *Who We Are.* Retrieved from https://esopstl.org/

Fatal Encounters. (2019). *A Step Towards Creating an Impartial, Comprehensive, and Searchable National Database of People Killed During Interactions with Law Enforcement.* Retrieved from https://fatalencounters.org/

Fanon, F. (1952). *Black Skin, White Masks.* (C. Farrington, Trans.). New York: Grove Publications.

Fanon, F (1967). *The Wretched of the Earth.* London: Penguin Books.

Federal Bureau of Investigations - Law Enforcement Bulletin. (2011). *Perspective: Peel's Legacy.* Retrieved from https://leb.fbi.gov/articles/perspective/perspective-peels-legacy

Federal Bureau of Investigations. (2019). *National Incident-Based Reporting System. (NIBRS)* Retrieved from https://www.fbi.gov/services/cjis/ucr/nibrs

Federal Bureau of Prisons. (2019). *Historical Information.* Retrieved from https://www.bop.gov/about/history/timeline.jsp

Feldman, B. (2014). *Armed Standoff Over Cattle Grazing Comes to an End.* The Atlantic. Retrieved from https://www.theatlantic.com/national/archive/2014/04/armed-standoff-over-cattle-grazing-comes-to-an-end/360594/

Feldman, J. (2015). *Public Health and the Policing of Black Lives.* Harvard Public Health Review. Retrieved from http://harvardpublichealthreview.org/public-health -and-the-policing-of-black-lives/

Ford, G. (2016). *Rulers Shocked by Dallas Attack: Black Folks Keep on Stepping.* Black Agenda Report. Retrieved from https://www.blackagendareport.com/after_dallas_blacks_keep _stepping

Franklin, F. E. (1962). The Failure of the Negro Intellectual. *The Negro Digest,* 11(4), 26–36.

Gabbidon, S., & Greene, H. (2013). *Race and Crime.* Thousands Oak, CA: Sage Publications.

Garvey, M. (1927). *The Tragedy of White Injustice.* New York, NY: Liberty Hall Publishers.

Gaskew, T. (2014a). *Rethinking Prison Reentry: Transforming Humiliation into Humility.* Lanham, MD: Lexington Books.

Gaskew, T. (2014b). The Policing of the Black American Male: Transforming Humiliation into Humility in Pursuit of Truth and Reconciliation. In I. Michelle Scott (ed.), *Crimes Against Humanity in the Land of the Free: Can a Truth and Reconciliation Process Heal Racial Conflict in America*? Santa Barbara, CA: ABC-CLIO Publishing.

Gaskew, T. (2016). *ADMJ 1449 – The United States of America vs. The United States of America* [Course syllabus]. Available from the University of Pittsburgh, Bradford, CourseWeb/Blackboard website: https://courseweb.pitt.edu/webapps / portal/ execute/tabs/tabAction?tab_tab_group_id=_2_1

Gaskew, T. (2018). Unfriending the Policing Culture: The Reawakened Black Consciousness. In Sandra E. Weissinger & Dwayne Mack (eds.), *Policing Black and Brown Bodies: Policing in the Age of Black Lives Matter.* Lanham, MD: Lexington-Rowman & Littlefield Books.

Gaskew, T. (2019). *ADMJ 1449 – Special Topics: Abolishing the Police.* [Course syllabus]. Available from the University of Pittsburgh, Bradford, CourseWeb/Blackboard website: https://courseweb.pitt.edu/webapps/portal/execute/tabs/tabAction?tab_tab_group_id=_2_1

Gaskew, T. (2020a). Stop Trying to Fix Policing: Lessons Learned from the Front Lines of Black Liberation. In Doug Irvin-Erickson & Emily Sample (eds.), *Building an Architecture of Peacebuilding in America.* London: Palgrave Macmillan.

Gaskew, T., & Thompson, S. (2020b). *The United States of America vs. the United States of America: Dissecting Systems of Oppression and White Supremacy.* Dialogues in Social Justice. College of Education, UNC Charlotte.

Gelderloos, P. (2018). *How Nonviolence Protects the State.* Boston, MA: Detritus Books.

Goldmacher, S. (2020). *Racial Justice Groups Flooded with Millions in Donations in Wake of Floyd Death.* The New York Times. Retrieved from https://www.nytimes.com/2020/06/14/us/politics/black-lives-matter-racism-donations.html

Government of the United Kingdom. (2012). *Freedom of Information Release: Definition of Policing by Consent.* Retrieved from https://www.gov.uk/government/publications/policing-by-consent/definition-of-policing-by-consent

Governing the Future of States and Localities. (2013). *Police Department Race and Ethnicity Demographic Data.* Retrieved from https://www.governing.com/gov-data/safety-justice/police-department-officer-demographics-minority-representati on.html

Greene, H., Gabbidon, S., & Wilson, S. (2018). Included? The Status of African American Scholars in the Discipline of Criminology and Criminal Justice Since 2004. *Journal of Criminal Justice Education, 29*(1), 96–115.

Hadden, S. (2001). *Slave Patrols: Law and Violence in Virginia and the Carolinas.* Harvard Cambridge, MA: University Press.

Hamaji, K., and Kumar, R. (2017). *Freedom to Thrive: Reimagining Safety & Security in Our Communities.* Retrieved from https://populardemocracy.org/sites/default/files/Freedom%20To%20Thrive%2C%20Higher%20Res%20Version.pdf ?utm_source=The+Appeal&utm_campaign=7e659f983a-EMAIL_CAMPAIGN _2018_08_09_04_14_COPY_01&utm_medium=email&utm_term=0_72df992d 8e659f983a-58426795

Haley, A. (1964). *The Autobiography of Malcolm X.* New York, NY: Ballantine Books.

Hampton, F. (1969a). *Power Anywhere Where There's People*, [Speech]. Delivered at the Olivet Baptist Church, Chicago.

Hampton, F. (1969b). *It's A Class Struggle Goddammit*, [Speech]. Delivered at Northern Illinois University, DeKalb.

Hampton, F. (1969c). *You Can Murder a Liberator, But You Can't Murder Liberation*, [Speech]. Delivered in Chicago.

Hass, J. (2010). *The Assassination of Fred Hampton: How the FBI and the Chicago Police Murdered a Black Panther.* Chicago, IL: Lawrence Hill Books.

Henderson. C. (1901). *An Introduction to the Study of the Dependent, Defective and Delinquent Classes.* Washington, DC: Health Press.

Henry, H. (1914). *The Police Control of the Slave in South Carolina.* Washington, DC: Negro Universities Press.

Hill, L. (2004). *The Deacons for Defense: Armed Resistance and the Civil Rights Movement.* Chapel Hill, NC: University of North Carolina Press.

Hilliard, A., Williams, L., & Damali, N. (1987). *The Teachings of Ptahhotep: The Oldest Book in the World.* Scotts Valley, CA: CreateSpace Publishing.

Hilliard, J. (2019). *New Study Examines the Tragic Relationship Between Police Officers and Suicide.* Retrieved from https://www.addictioncenter.com/news/2019 /09/police-at-highest-risk-for-suicide-than-any-profession/

Hoekstra, M., & Sloan, C. (2020). *Does Race Matter for Police Use of Force? Evidence from 911 Calls.* The National Bureau of Economic Research. Working Paper No. 26774. Retrieved from https://www.nber.org/

Hoffman, F. (1896). *Race Traits and Tendencies of the American Negro.* Nashville, TN: American Economic Association.

Hotep. A. (2016). *The Book of Ma'at.* Middletown, DE: The Guardians of Ma'at University.

Huey P. Newton Gun Club. (2019). *Mission Statement and Local Objectives.* Retrieved from https://hueypnewtongunclub.org/home

Jackson, G. (1970). *Soledad Brother.* New York, NY: Bantam Books.

Johnson, N. (2014). *Negroes and the Gun: The Black Tradition of Arms*. Buffalo: Prometheus Books.

Jones, N. (1989). *Born a Child of Freedom, Yet a Slave: Mechanisms of Control and Strategies of Resistance in Antebellum South Carolina*. Middletown, CT: Wesleyan University Press.

Joseph, P. (2007). *Waiting 'Til the Midnight Hour: A Narrative History of Black Power in America*. New York: Griffin.

Kambon, M. (2013). *To Serve the People: Black Riders Liberation Party, New Generation Black Panther Party for Self-Defense*. Retrieved from https://sfbayvi ew.com/2013/09/to-serve-the-people-black-riders-liberation-party-new-genera tion-black-panther-party-for-self-defense/

Kamene, K. H. (2019). *Spirituality Before Religions: Spirituality is Unseen Science . . . Science is Seen Spirituality*. Scotts Valley, CA: CreateSpace Publishing

Karade, B. I., (1994). *The Handbook of Yoruba Religious Concepts*. New York: Weiser Books.

Karenga, M. (2010) *Introduction to Black Studies*. Los Angeles, CA: University of Sankore Press.

Kefing, O. (2016). *Micah Xavier: Our African Patriot!* Burning Spear News. Retrieved from https://www.theburningspear.com/2016/08/MICAH-XAVIER-OU R-AFRICAN-PATRIOT

Kessler, R. (2017). *Inside the White House: The Hidden Lives of the Modern Presidents and the Secrets of the World's Most Powerful Institution*. New York, NY: Gallery Books.

King, M. L. (1967). *The Three Evils of Society*, [Speech]. Delivered at the National Conference on New Politics, Chicago.

King, M. L. (1968). *Why We Can't Wait*. London: Signet Publications.

King, S. K. (1990). *Urban Shaman: A Handbook for Personal and Planetary Transformation Based on the Hawaiian Way of the Adventure*. New York, NY: Touchstone Publishing.

Kufuor, O. (2015). *The Black Bible of Science: The Kemet Version*. Morrisville, NC: Lulu Publications.

Kopel, D., & Greenlee, J. (2017). *The Racist Origin of Gun Control Laws*. The Hill. Retrieved from https://thehill.com/blogs/pundits-blog/civil-rights/347324-the-ra cist-origin-of-gun-control-laws

Law Enforcement Action Partnership. (2019). *Sir Robert Peel's Policing Principles*. Retrieved from https://lawenforcementactionpartnership.org/peel-policing-princip les/

Levin, S. (2016). *Oregon Standoff Tension Mounts as so-called '3%' Groups Refuse to Leave*. Retrieved from https://www.theguardian.com/us-news/2016/jan/10/or egon-standoff-three-percenter-groups

Lombroso, C. (1876). *Criminal Man*. Italy: University of Turin.

Madison, D. S. (2012). *Critical Ethnography: Methods, Ethics, and Performance*. Thousand Oaks, CA: Sage Publications.

Memnon, R. (2015). *Police Brutality and Black Self Defense*. Black Star News. Retrieved from http://www.blackstarnews.com/blog/police-brutality-and-black -self-defense.html

McCarthy, N. (2017). *How Much Do U.S. Cities Spend Every Year on Policing?* Forbes. Retrieved from https://www.forbes.com/sites/niallmccarthy/2017/08/07/how-much-do-u-s-cities-spend-every-year-on-policing-infographic/

Miller, D. A. H. (2011). Retail Rebellion and the Second Amendment. *Indiana Law Journal, 86*(3), Article 5.

Miller, D. A. H., & Blocher, J. (2018). *The Positive Second Amendment: Rights, Regulation, and the Future of Heller.* Cambridge, UK: Cambridge University Press.

Mngxitama, A. (2016). *Micah Xavier Johnson the martyr of BLACK people the world over.* Black Opinion. Retrieved from https://blackopinion.co.za/2016/07/10/micah-xavier-johnson-martyr-black-people-world/

MPD150. (2019a). *MPD150's Five Essential Findings.* Retrieved from https://www.mpd150.com/mpd150s-five-essential-findings/

MPD150. (2019b). *Enough is Enough: A 150 Year Performance Review of the Minneapolis Police Department.* Retrieved from https://www.mpd150.com/wp-content/themes/mpd150/assets/mpd150_report.pdf

Muhammad, E. (1965). *Message to the Blackman in America.* Irving, TX: Secretarius Memps Publications.

Muhammad, K. (2010). *The Condemnation of Blackness: Race, Crime, and the Making of Urban America.* Cambridge, MA: Harvard University Press.

Muncey, T. (2010). *Creating Autoethnographies.* Thousand Oaks, CA: Sage Publications. Sage Publications.

Muntaqim, J. (1997). *On the Black Liberation Army.* Montreal, QC: Montreal Anarchist Black Cross.

Muntaqim, J. (2010). *We Are Our Own Liberators.* Chicago, IL: Arissa Publishing.

Murray, A. (1973). White Norms, Black Deviation. In Joyce Ladner (ed.), *The Death of White Sociology.* Baltimore, MD: Black Classic Press.

National African American Gun Association. (2019). *Black Gun History.* Retrieved from https://naaga.co/

National Archives. (2019). *Black Power Records RG 65 - Records of the Federal Bureau of Investigation.* Retrieved from https://www.archives.gov/research/african-americans/record-groups/rg-065-fbi-class157.html

National Center for Women & Policing. (2019). *Police Family Violence Fact Sheet.* Retrieved from http://womenandpolicing.com/violenceFS.asp#notes

National Museum of Ireland. (2019). *Preserving the Peace: An Exhibition Exploring Policing in Ireland from 1814 Up Until the Present Day.* Retrieved from https://www.museum.ie/Country-Life/Exhibitions/Previous-Exhibitions/Preserving-the-Peace

Newton, H. (1972). *To Die for the People.* New York: Random House Publishing.

New York City Department of Public Health and Mental Hygiene. (2019). *Criminal Justice Action Kit.* Retrieved from https://www1.nyc.gov/site/doh/providers/resources/public-health-action-kits-criminal-justice-involvement.page

New York City Police Pension Fund (2020). Serving the Finest. Retrieved from https://www1.nyc.gov/html/nycppf/html/home/home.shtml

Nguyen, J. (2020). *Police departments have Spent Millions in Overtime During Protests.* Retrieved from https://www.marketplace.org/2020/07/03/police-departments-have-spent-millions-in-overtime-during-protests/

Nichodemus, Y. N. (2013). *Theory of African Metaphysics*. Scotts Valley, CA: CreateSpace Publishing.

Nicholson, B. (1994). Legal Borrowing and the Origins of Slave Law in the British Colonies. *The American Journal of Legal History*, *38*(1), 51.

Nkrumah, K. (1968). *Handbook of Revolutionary Warfare*. Bedford, UK: Panaf Books.

Nobles, W. W. (1972). *African Philosophy: Foundation for Black Psychology*. In R. L. Jones (ed.), *Black Psychology*. New York, NY: Harper & Row.

Nobles, W. W. (1985). *Africanity and the Black Family: The Development of a Theoretical Model*. Oakland, CA: A Black Family Institute Publication.

Nobles, W. W. (1986). Ancient Egyptian Thought and the Renaissance of African (Black) Psychology. In Maulana Karenga & Jacob Carruthers (eds.), *Kemet and the African Worldview*. Los Angeles, CA: University of Sankore Press.

Nobles, W. W. (2000). *Working with African American People*. Cultural Groundings, Volume I: Los Angeles, CA: University of Sankore Press.

Obenga, T. (2015). *African Philosophy*. Tampa, FL: Brawtley Press.

Office of the New York City Comptroller. (2018). *Claims Report: Fiscal year 2017*. Retrieved from https://comptroller.nyc.gov/wp-content/uploads/documents/Claims-Report-FY-2017.pdf

Official Reports of the Supreme Court. (2010). Volume 561 U.S. – Part 1, Pages 76; 100020. Washington, DC: U.S. Government Publication.

Oliver, W. (2019). *August Vollmer: The Father of American Policing*. Durham, NC: Carolina Academic Press.

Olugbala, D. (2017). *Black Control of the Police is a Democratic Right*. Retrieved from https://www.blackagendareport.com/black-control-police-democratic-right

Olugbala, D. (2019a). *Black is Back Coalition: Black Community Control of Police in Philly*. Retrieved from https://www.theburningspear.com/2019/01/Black-is-Back-Coalition-Black-Community-Control-of-Police

Olugbala, D. (2019b). *BCCP Working Group Leader Interview: The Black Agenda Report*. Retrieved from https://soundcloud.com/user-208734627/sets/black-agenda-radio-week-of-82

Olusoga, D. (2015). *The History of British Slave Ownership has been Buried: Now its Scale Can Be Revealed*. Retrieved from https://www.theguardian.com/world/2015/jul/12/british- history-slavery-buried-scale-revealed

O'Reilly, K. (1991). *Racial Matters: The FBI's Secret File on Black America, 196972*. New York, NY: The Free Press.

Page-Balkcom, L. (2015). *MA'AT 42 Plus GOD: Common Sense Approach Ideas to Living a Prosperous Life in Truth, Justice, Order, Balance and Love*. Santa Barbara, CA: CreateSpace Publishing.

Pearson v. Callahan, 555 U.S. 223, 231 (2009).

Pew Research Center. (2019). *Behind the Badge: Inside America's Police Departments*. Retrieved from https://www.pewsocialtrends.org/2017/01/11/inside-americas-police-departments/

Police Officers. (2018). *Diversity*. Retrieved from https://datausa.io/profile/soc/police-officers#about

Revealing Histories: Remembering Slavery. (2019). *Why Was Cotton So Important in North West England?* Retrieved from http://revealinghistories.org.uk/why-was-cotton-so-important-in-north-west-england.html

Robinson, C. (1983). *Black Marxism: The Making of the Black Radical Tradition.* London: Zep Press.

Rosen, L. (2016). *The Creation of the Uniform Crime Report: The Role of Social Science.* Cambridge, UK: Cambridge University Press.

Saad, L. (2019). *What Percentage of Americans Own Guns?* Gallup. Retrieved from https://news.gallup.com/poll/264932/percentage-americans-own-guns.aspx

Sanders, K. (2015). A Reason to Resist: The Use of Deadly Force in Aiding Victims of Unlawful Police Aggression. *San Diego Law Review, 52*(3), Article 6.

Sankara, T. (1988). *Thomas Sankara Speaks: The Burkina Faso Revolution 198987.* Atlanta, GA: Pathfinder Publications.

Sayles, J. (2010). *Meditations on Frantz Fanon's Wretched of the Earth: New Afrikan Revolutionary Writing.* London: Kersplebedeb.

Schoatz, R. (2013). *Maroon the Implacable.* Oakland, CA: PM Press.

Scott, J. (2018). *The Common Wind: Afro-American Currents in the Age of the Haitian Revolution.* Brooklyn, NY: Verso.

Shabazz, M. (April 8, 1964). *The Black Revolution*, [Speech]. Delivered in New York City.

Shakur, A. (1987). *Assata: An Autobiography.* Chicago, IL: Lawrence Hill Books

Shiffer, A. (2017). *Abolish the Police, Now! An interview Mohamed Shehk from Critical Resistance on What We Mean When We Say Abolish Police and Prisons.* Retrieved from https://www.okayafrica.com/how-to-abolish-police-prisons/

Short, R. (2016). *Micah Xavier Johnson: Made in America, a Failed Human Rights State.* Black Agenda Report. Retrieved from https://blackagendareport.com/index.php/us _failed_human_rights_state

Siedlak, M. J. (2016). *Seven African Powers: The Orishas.* New York: Oshun Publications LLC.

Siegal, I., & Worrall, J. (2019). *Introduction to Criminal Justice* (16th edition). Boston, MA: Centage Publishing.

Smith, A. L. (2015). *Black Open Carry: The Armed African-Americans Patrolling Dallas.* Retrieved from https://www.texasstandard.org/stories/black-open-carry-the-armed-african-americans-patrolling-dallas/

Somé, M. P. (1997). *Ritual: Power, Healing and Community.* New York: Penguin Books.

Somé, M. P. (1998). *The Healing Wisdom of Africa: Finding Life Purpose Through Nature, Ritual, and Community.* New York: Putnam Books.

Somé, S. (2000). *The Spirit of Intimacy: Ancient African Teachings in the Ways of Relationships.* New York: William Morrow Paperbacks.

Southern Poverty Law Center. (2014). *War in the West: The Bundy Ranch Standoff and the American Radical Right.* Retrieved from https://www.splcenter.org/2014 0709/war-west-bundy-ranch-standoff-and-american-radical-right

Street, P. (2016). *Micah Xavier Johnson and Gavin Long: Seventeen Reasons.* Black Agenda Report. Retrieved from https://www.blackagendareport.com/black_vet_s nipers_reasons

Stop Police Terror Project. (2019a). *Stop Police Terror Project DC-Stands on These Basic Principles.* Retrieved from https://www.sptdc.com/who-we-are

Stop Police Terror Project. (2019b). *Get Informed.* Retrieved from https://www.sptdc .com/understand-the-problem-1

Sublette, N. (2017). *The American Slave Coast: A History of the Slave-Breeding Industry.* Chicago, IL: Lawrence Hill Books.

Summers, A. (2012). The Secret Life of J Edgar Hoover. *The Guardian.* Retrieved from https://www.theguardian.com/film/2012/jan/01/j-edgar-hoover-secret-fbi

The Black Panther. (1967). *What We Want Now, What We Believe.* Black Community News Service. Volume I, Number 6. The Black Panther Party for Self Defense.

The Council of the City of New York. (2019). *Report of the Finance Division on the Fiscal 2019 Preliminary Budget; The Fiscal 2018 Preliminary Mayor's Management Report for the New York Police Department.* Retrieved from https:/ /council.nyc.gov/budget/wp-content/uploads/sites/54/2018/03/FY19-New-York-P olice-Department.pdf

The President's Commission on Law Enforcement and Administration of Justice. (1967). *The Challenge of Crime in a Free Society.* Retrieved from https://www.ncj rs.gov/pdffiles1/nij/42.pdf

The Seattle Times. (2019). *Capital-B 'Black' Becomes Standard Usage at The Seattle Times.* Retrieved from https://www.seattletimes.com/seattle-news/capital-b-black -becomes-standard-usage-at-the-seattle-times/?amp=1&__twitter_impression=true

The Sentencing Project. (2015). *Black Lives Matter: Eliminating Racial Inequity in the Criminal Justice System.* Retrieved from http://sentencingproject.org/wp- conte nt/uploads/2015/11/Black-Lives-Matter.pdf

The Sentencing Project. (2017). *Race & Justice News: One-Third of Black Men Have Felony Convictions.* Retrieved from https://www.sentencingproject.org/news/5593/

The Young Turks. (2014). *Militia Member Threatens to Kill Cops.* Retrieved from https://youtu.be/J2crIzQXkO4

Thompson, A. (2006). *Flight to Freedom: African Runaways and Maroons in the Americas.* West Indies: University Press of West Indies.

Thompson, S. (2015). *The United States of America vs. the United States of America* [Lecture Notes]. University of Pittsburgh, Bradford, ADMJ 1449. University of Pittsburgh Press.

Ture, K. (1964). *Stokely Carmichael - Civil Rights Speech.* [Video File]. Retrieved from https://www.biography.com/video/stokely-carmichael-civil-rights-speech -12508227919

Ture, K. (1966). *Black Power Speech.* [Video File]. Retrieved from https://youtu.be/ _2Dmd9g_GDQ

Ture, K. (1967a). *Black Power: The Politics of Liberation.* New York: Vintage Books.

Ture, K. (1967b). *Stokely Carmichael "We Ain't Going" Speech.* [Video File]. Retrieved from https://youtu.be/HKP5_qyGs8c

Ture, K. (1967c). *Stokely Carmichael - Passive Boycotts.* [Video File]. Retrieved from https://youtu.be/Q_QbWDoJBvk

Ture, K. (1970). *Committee on the Judiciary: United States Senate,* [Speech]. Delivered at Washington, D.C.

Ture, K. (1971). *From Black Power to Pan-Africanism,* [Speech]. Delivered at Whittier College, California.

Ture, K. (1972). *Stokely Carmichael Lecture at Howard University.* [Video File]. Retrieved from https://youtu.be/mhRujWQy5Tk

Ture, K. (1973). *Stokely Carmichael speaking at UCLA.* [Video File]. Retrieved from https://youtu.be/9B3pmRlNaP4

Ture, K. (1986). *Eyes on the Prize.* [Video File]. Retrieved from https://youtu.be /7R_Qd9gA

Ture, K. (1990). *Kwame Ture at University of Illinois.* [Video File]. Retrieved from https://youtu.be/c6ZWJT3B3r0

Ture, K. (1992). *Kwame Ture speaks at Florida International University in Miami.* [Video File]. Retrieved from https://youtu.be/bN8oq7lF9FA

Ture, K. (1996a). *African Culture.* [Video File]. Retrieved from https://youtu.be/ BoLTJJy7wZk

Ture, K. (1996b). *Kwame Ture Converting the Unconscious to Conscious.* [Video File]. Retrieved from https://youtu.be/4Y3KQbQF3Qk

Ture, K. (1996c). *No Revolution Without Organization.* [Video File]. Retrieved from https://youtu.be/ROew63_7sg4

Ture, K. (1997a). *The FBI and CIA.* [Video File]. Retrieved from https://youtu.be/ YCTMT62DIIM

Ture, K. (1997b). *Stokely Carmichael on Nonviolence.* [Video File]. Retrieved from https://youtu.be/_klzg5kkbhM

Ture, K. (1997c). *Kwame Ture at Cheyney University.* [Video File]. Retrieved from https://youtu.be/AiewiXVAqW8

Ture, K. (1997d). *Pan Afrikanism and the New World Order.* [Video File]. Retrieved from https://youtu.be/6qlPecr3zZk

Ture, K. (1998). *Kwame Ture's Last Fire Side Chat from the Mecca-Howard.* [Video File]. Retrieved from https://youtu.be/aW45PbSXyMM

Ture, K., & Ekwueme, M. (2003). *Ready for Revolution: The Life and Struggles of Stokely Carmichael {Kwame Ture}.* New York, NY: Scribner Press.

UK Parliament Archives. (2019). *Parliament and the British Slave Trade 160833-Petition from Manufacturers and Merchants of Manchester against the Foreign Slave Trade Abolition Bill.* Retrieved from https://www.parliament.uk /about/living-heritage/transformingsociety/tradeindustry/slavetrade/from-the-par liamentary-collections/the-british-slave-trade/petition-against-the-foreign-slave-tra de-abolition-bill-page-1/

Umoja, A. O. (2014). *We Will Shoot Back.* New York, NY: NYU Press.

University of Chicago. (2019). *NORC and the University of Chicago.* Retrieved from http://www.norc.org/About/Pages/university-of-chicago-affiliation.aspx

University of Pittsburgh. (2019). *Spring 2019 - Tony Gaskew ADMJ 1449 SPECIAL TOPICS IN COURTS - 2010 Lecture*. OMET 2194-Teaching Survey Spring 2019. Retrieved from https://teaching.pitt.edu/omet/

U. S. Census Bureau. (2019). *1890 Overview*. Retrieved from https://www.census.gov/history/www/through_the_decades/overview/1890.html

U.S. Department of Education, National Center for Education Statistics. (2019). *Digest of Education Statistics, 2017*. Retrieved from https://nces.ed.gov/fastfacts/display.asp?id=73

U.S. Department of Justice, Programs Bureau of Justice Statistics. (2015). *Local Police Departments, 2013: Personnel, Policies, and Practices*. Retrieved from https://www.bjs.gov/content/pub/pdf/lpd13ppp.pdf

U.S. Department of Justice, Office of Justice Programs, Bureau of Justice Statistics (2018). *Contacts Between Police and the Public, 2015*. Retrieved from https://www.bjs.gov/content/pub/pdf/cpp15.pdf

U. S. Department of Justice. Federal Bureau of Investigation. *Uniform Crime Reports, 193959. ICPSR03666-v1* [Data file]. Ann Arbor, MI: Inter-university Consortium for Political and Social Research.

Walters, K. (2015). *American Slave Revolts and Conspiracies*. Santa Barbara, CA: ABC-CLIO Publishing.

Welsing, F. (1992). *The Isis Papers: The Keys to the Colors*. New York: CW Publishing.

West, C. (2001). *Race Matters* (2nd edition). New York, NY: Vintage Press.

Williams, A. (2000). *Being Black: Zen and the Art of Living with Fearlessness and Grace*. New York, NY: Penguin Compass Press.

Williams, A., Owens, L., & Syedullah, J. (2016). *Radical Dharma: Talking Race, Love, and Liberation*. Berkeley, CA: North Atlantic Books.

Williams, C. (1971). *The Destruction of Black Civilization*. Chicago, IL: Third World Press.

Williams, R. F. (1962). *Negroes with Guns*. Eastford, CT: Martino Publishing.

Wilson, A. (1998). *Blueprint for Black Power*. Brooklyn, NY: Afrikan World Infosystems.

Wood, B. (1997). *The Origins of American Slavery: Freedom and Bondage in the English Colonies*. New York, NY: Hill and Wang.

Woodson, C. G. (1933). *The Mis-Education of the Negro*. Trenton, NJ: Africa World Press.

Yakubu, O. Y. (1981). *On Transforming the Colonial and Criminal Mentality,* in Notes from a New Afrikan P.O.W. Journal, Book 7. Chicago, IL: Spear and Shield Publications.

Zuberi, T., & Bonilla-Silva, E. (2008). Toward a Definition of White Logic and White Methods. In T. Zuberi, & E. Bonilla-Silva (eds.), *White Logic, White Methods: Racism and Methodology*. Lanham, MD: Rowman & Littlefield Publishers.

Index

About the Author

Tony Gaskew, PhD, is professor of Criminal Justice, Affiliate Faculty of Africana Studies, director of the Criminal Justice Program, and founding director of the nationally recognized Prison Education Program at the University of Pittsburgh, Bradford. As a critical race theorist, his research examines the oppressive nature of policing, within the Black experience in America, the Black Power Movement, and the Black radical tradition. His award-winning book *Rethinking Prison Reentry: Transforming Humiliation into Humility* shifted the pedagogical language of building a Black resistance consciousness within higher education inside prisons. As a Fulbright-Hays scholar in Kemet, his critical autoethnographic insights have led to the publication of dozens of journal articles, book chapters, and books, including this book, *Stop Trying to Fix Policing: Lessons Learned from the Front Lines of Black Liberation* (Lexington-Rowman & Littlefield), which examines police abolition through the eyes of the Black radical tradition. Dr. Gaskew is widely considered one of the leading subject-matter experts in the country regarding the impact of policing on the Black diaspora in America.

www.ingramcontent.com/pod-product-compliance
Lightning Source LLC
Chambersburg PA
CBHW022326280326
41932CB00010B/1246